UMD's Rare and Remarkable

UMD's Rare and Remarkable

Stories from the Past

University of Minnesota Duluth

Contents

The Rare and Remarkable: Stories from the Past

The following is a collection of stories spanning 13 decades in celebration of UMD's 125th Anniversary. As the year 2020 progressed, UMD posted accounts on a website and in the Alumni E-Newsletter about UMD's rare and remarkable history. UMD's past is tightly woven into the history of the city and the history of Minnesota itself. Learn how Duluth streets, Minnesota towns, and areas of the nation still hold fragments left behind as the campus grew. There is excitement in the adventures of the people that made up UMD. Enjoy this account of the university as it grew on its place overlooking Lake Superior.

These stories were edited by Cheryl Reitan. The individual chapters were written by Cheryl Reitan, UMD staff, and UMD students from January 2020 to January 2021.

1.

Honoring Our History

Transforming leaders and empowering communities.

The university acknowledges that the University of Minnesota Duluth resides on what has always been indigenous lands. In Fall 2019, UMD adopted a formal Land Acknowledgement stating that the campus occupies traditional, ancestral, and contemporary lands of indigenous people. As UMD launches into the celebration of 125 years as an educational institution, it recognizes the deep history and the enduring relationship that exists between indigenous peoples and their traditional territories.

Wayne Dupuis '87, the environmental program manager for the Fond du Lac Band of Lake Superior Chippewa, shared insights about the Duluth that existed hundreds of years ago. "The whole hillside was covered in white pine," he says. Many of the trees were over 400 years old growing to heights of 150 feet.

"The area that is now Duluth was called Onigamiising, or the place of the small portage. The creeks were called ziibiins." In the creek that runs through campus, trout climbed uphill from Lake Superior. The Ojibwe name of Lake Superior is Gichigami.

The land now occupied by UMD was home to bear, moose, rabbit, and deer. Porcupine, mink, marten, fisher, and partridge were plentiful. Nearby maples provided maple syrup, and birch bark yielded the material to make canoes and shelters.

Anishinaabe people lived on the shores of Lake Superior in Duluth and the surrounding areas. This place was and is of great meaning to the Anishinaabe people.

Students, Staff, and Faculty Contributions at UMD

Programming for American Indian students launched in response to requests by local Anishinaabe students in the late 1960s. They wanted American Indian perspectives included as a part of the courses being offered at UMD. Around that same time, the young students formed the university-wide Anishinaabe Club, which through the years has continued its historical, grassroots relationship with the Department of American Indian Studies, alumni, and the community. In recent years, the students decided to change the name of the club to the Indigenous Student Organization (ISO).

Several faculty, staff, and students advocated for and an increased American Indian presence at UMD. Ruth Myers, known as the "grandmother of American Indian Education in Minnesota," started working in the UMD Department of Education in 1973.

In the early 1980s, Myers joined the staff of the University of Minnesota Medical School-Duluth Campus. She started many UMD programs for American Indian students, including the Center for American Indian and Minority Health in the School of Medicine-Duluth Campus. Myers also founded the Center for

Indigenous Education in the Department of Education, and the center was named in her honor.

The university has added expanded American Indian program offerings, and each year American Indian students earn degrees from majors across UMD's five colleges.

American Indian Studies at UMD has grown from a single class to a program then a department. Since 1979, students have been able to complete a minor, and in 1994 the Bachelor of Arts major was added. The department works to educate students, colleagues, and the public about tribal sovereignty, American Indian cultures, and both the historic and contemporary experiences of Native peoples and nations.

American Indian Studies faculty regularly share their research findings and creative works. The department collaborates with MN DOT to offer the Minnesota Tribal-State Relations Training, which prepares state agency employees with the knowledge and tools to consult with American Indian nations on matters of mutual interest.

In addition, students can earn a B.A. in American Indian Studies as well as in Tribal Administration and Governance. Graduate programs include the Masters of Tribal Administration and Governance (MTAG) and Tribal Resource and Environmental Stewardship (MTRES).

Past and Future

UMD looks back at its history through activities such as the Land Acknowledgement, and it also looks forward toward more inclusive programming. It has made a commitment to fostering and supporting American Indian culture during its 125th anniversary year and will continue for years to come.

by Cheryl Reitan

——

The banner photograph at the beginning of this chapter is from the map: Wellge, H, J. J Stoner, and Beck & Pauli. View of Duluth, Minn. [Madison, Wis., J. J. Stoner, 1883].

2.

Creating a Duluth Campus

Higher education serves a large and growing population.

Robert E. Denfeld, who was superintendent of the Duluth public schools from 1885 to 1916, was an early vocal proponent of the State Normal School at Duluth (Duluth Normal School).

In an article written two years before the legislature voted to establish the school, he argued against his opponents in favor of the school. The January 19, 1893 Duluth Evening Herald reported that "Superintendent Denfeld is exceedingly interested in the normal school question."

Denfeld supported a bill to create a Duluth Normal School which was penned by James A. Boggs, the legislator from Cook, Lake, and St. Louis counties. That appropriation came from Boggs'

Public Buildings Committee, which sought $100,000 for the erection of a state school building in Duluth.

According to the Herald, Denfeld "was exerting himself to the utmost to get an appropriation from the legislature for the purpose." Denfeld recognized that the population of Minnesota and Duluth was growing and more teachers were urgently needed.

Between 1880 and 1890 the population of Minnesota grew nearly 530,000, and between 1890 and 1900 it grew another 440,000, primarily in urban areas. Denfeld had cause for alarm.

He argued vehemently for the appropriation. "The school at St. Cloud is the nearest one to Duluth, and if we had a normal here, there would be a large number of pupils who would attend that can not go to St. Cloud," he said. "If Duluth had a normal, it would doubtless draw many pupils from other sections. Our large and growing population demands that it should be here."

Denfeld and the other supporters were eventually met with success. The legislature passed the authorization. According to the April 3, 1895 *Duluth Evening Herald*, Governor David. M. Clough signed the Normal School into creation. The headline read, "SCHOOL! Governor Approved Duluth Normal School…"

It took several more years to secure funding for the Normal School and in 1901, during construction, the school burned down. In 1902, a second building was erected. On September 2, 1902, the first class was admitted under the leadership of Dr. E.W. Bohannon, the first Duluth Normal School president.

by Cheryl Reitan

———

The banner photograph at the beginning of the chapter is of the second Minnesota State Capitol in St. Paul is from the Minnesota Historical Society.

3.

Trolley Cars to the Rescue

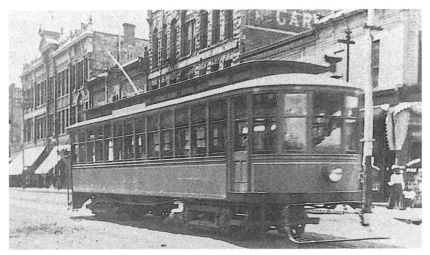

The first students are provided with an easy commute.

A Chronology of UMD Events, a history document written by Clarence Anderson, a former UMD news service director, tells an early story. Before the first State Normal School at Duluth (Duluth Normal School) student set foot on campus, a new trolley car line was laid. The tracks went up the hill on 24th Avenue East from the Superior Street trolley car line to Fourth Street, allowing the future students easy access to campus.

Getting the Students to Class

Anderson's document described the bareness of the neighborhood on Duluth's east hillside, "There were no paved streets or avenues in the vicinity... A boardwalk was laid over the muddy ground from the streetcar to the school." The students came from all over, including the large residential area in the western part of the city. It wouldn't be until 1906 when the first dormitory, Washburn Hall, would be built.

The First Buildings

After finally securing financing from the legislature for a Duluth Normal School building, work began in 1900. Tragically, before it was completed, the building was destroyed by fire in February 1901.

In spite of the fire, the state normal school board did not waver in their effort to construct the new school building. Their building committee received assistance from the City of Duluth for water supply, sewer, and gas mains and construction commenced. According to the Board of Education reports, the building had, "grounds graded, concrete floors laid in the basement... the structure equipped with furniture, and the school was opened in a successful manner with a good attendance for occupancy on September 2, 1902."

The First Class

It took Dr. E. W. Bohannon, the first Duluth Normal School president, more than a year to gather that inaugural class. Beginning enrollment was 91 young women, and the faculty numbered 10 members.

Transportation helped. In addition to the future teachers, elementary school children had to get to their "laboratory classrooms" at the Duluth Normal School. "There were few residences within walking distance, and many elementary school children came by horse-drawn bus or by horseback," wrote Anderson. "Occasionally a stray cow would be attracted to the new lawn, only to be rounded up and impounded at the rear of the building."

Some of the students brought in credits from other schools, so in June 1903, the Duluth Normal School was able to see seven women graduate. The success of the first graduates and the new school was certainly due, in part, to those first four blocks of trolley car tracks and the Duluth Street Car Railway.

by Cheryl Reitan

———

The banner photo at the beginning of the chapter shows one of the new trolley cars purchased in 1902 for the expanding streetcar system. The photo is included in the book Twin Ports by Trolley: The Streetcar Era in Duluth-Superior *by Aaron Isaacs. The quotes in the story came from* A Chronology of UMD Events: 1895-1984, *a document written by Clarence Anderson, University Relations Representative, and added by other UMD staff members.*

4.

Arts and Crafts: Early Years

A 1907 story reveals an emphasis on arts in the home.

From the beginning, the State Normal School at Duluth (Duluth Normal School) kept up with the times. It embraced the values of the Arts and Crafts movement, which originated decades earlier in England. London artist William Morris and others created beautiful and useful home items as a reaction to the Industrial Revolution and the exhausting factory labor suffered by workers. Normal School teachers took the principals of Arts and Crafts to heart, along with many in the nation's education system.

In Duluth, the normal school student teachers taught children to work with wood, metal, leather, and raffia (grasses). A June 9, 1907. Duluth News Tribune article detailed the work to be displayed at an Arts and Crafts public exhibit in Duluth. The writer says, "Every piece of work done… is a piece of genuine expression on the part of the pupil."

The article goes on to praise the teacher of the student teachers, "Miss Hellman Bainbridge has… most progressive theories as to its application… Her work has proven… the practicability of her ideas and the wonderful possibilities of industrial work." The enthusiastic writer continues, "Every girl… has gone out… with new ideas of beauty, [and] new standards for household decoration and adornment."

The reader is reminded that only women were taught at the Normal School. "The girls are going to teach in the schools of the state, to form and reform the taste of the coming generation…[and] in the final reckoning, they will be the makers of homes…"

There's a jab at old-fashioned Victorian style as the writer continues, [The girls will be] "the principal factors in the elimination of ornate furniture, daring pictures and gilded gewgaws that make the average American home a thing of ugliness and useless expenditures." The newspaper article doesn't mention where in Duluth the 1907 Arts and Crafts Exhibit was held, but it does mention other participants. "There will be loan exhibits from other cities of various kinds of artistic handiwork and lectures by such well-known authorities as Forrest Emerson Mann of the Grand Rapids School of Applied Arts and George Weitbrecht of the Mechanics Arts High School of St. Paul."

In fact, George Weitbrecht was well-known for his respected school. It was the first high school in the Upper Midwest to combine manual training with traditional academic curricula.

In addition to tile work and weaving, the newspaper writer was impressed by the playhouse (pictured above), the work of the first and second grades under the charge of student-teacher Miss Florence Ely. "These children… made a plan for the playhouse, drawing an excellent design... and using definite measurements for doors and windows."

The article goes on to compliment, "rooms furnished with most ingenious furniture... and pretty rugs on the floor," all made by the children.

Today's readers are sure to agree with this writer from a century ago. The Duluth Normal School did some very impressive work, beginning in its earliest years.

by Cheryl Reitan

———

A scrapbook containing an original copy of the June 9, 1907 Duluth News Tribune *article is housed in the Duluth Public Library. The two-page article details the exhibit, along with a few original photographs. The photos above of the playhouse, the artwork, and the Duluth Normal School in 1907 are included in the scrapbook. A transcript of the article and copies of the photographs are located in the Archives and Special Collections, Kathryn A. Martin Library, University of Minnesota Duluth.*

5.

Party at the Washburn Home

Jed L. Washburn: Gracious host and great philanthropist.

Attorney Jed L. Washburn heavily influenced the development of the State Normal School at Duluth (Duluth Normal School). He was an advocate for education; due to his many donations and active commitment to the Normal School, he was appointed resident director from 1903 to 1920. Both Washburn and his wife, Alma, were prominent figures in education, and they often opened their home to the students and faculty from the Duluth Normal School for entertaining.

Washburn was born on December 26, 1856 in Indiana. After deciding to reside in Duluth in 1890, he spent most of his time involved in public and business affairs. He was a member of

Duluth's Board of Education from 1900 to 1907, and he played a key role in the development of Jay Cooke State Park.

Always civically and socially active, Washburn held memberships in the Kitchi Gammi Club, Northland Country Club, and the Duluth Curling Club. He was a well-known lawyer, banker, and businessman who had the trust of most in Duluth. For instance, when an ambassador from Great Britain, James Bryce, came to visit Duluth, Washburn was chosen to deliver an address on behalf of the entire city.

The Host

Alma and Jed opened their home for parties and dances on many occasions. Their annual party for graduating seniors and faculty was a special highlight. The large rooms were filled with young women from the Duluth Normal School and their dates. One can imagine seeing a talented young person playing music on the piano or hearing the sounds of a Victrola.

Their home, which once stood at 101 Oxford Avenue, was just off Woodland Avenue in the Hunter's Park neighborhood. They lived in the house beginning in 1894. It featured a round tower, a third-floor wall with patterned shingles, and a porch that encircled a corner of the first floor. After the passing of Washburn in 1931 and his wife in 1943, their home stood vacant and was demolished in 1946.

The Philanthropist

The first dormitory for women at the Duluth Normal School, Washburn Hall, was named after Washburn. He donated funds for the construction of the building and gave support to President Bohannon. Washburn was known for beautifying the campus at his own expense. This can be seen in the wonderful design of Washburn Hall, which still stands to this day. Washburn participated in the day-to-day operation of the school. He was frequently on campus visiting classes and giving talks on education as well as his lifelong interest in history.

According to the October 28, 1905 Duluth News Tribune, Washburn donated the Duluth Normal School site, provided the school with equipment for its manual training department, and spent a great deal of time overseeing the building's construction. The Duluth Public School, Washburn Elementary, was also named after him.

"No one knew the extent of his benefactions," stated John G. Williams, who wrote a biography on Washburn.

by Ellie Mercil

——

The banner is photo at the beginning of the chapter is of the Washburn home is courtesy of the Duluth Public Library.

6.

The Aftermath of the 1918 Fire

The Duluth Normal School personnel pitch in to save lives.

The State Normal School at Duluth (Duluth Normal School) felt the devastating effects of both the fire of 1918 and the influenza pandemic which followed. The 1918 fire originated from sparks along the Cloquet train tracks and burned from October 10-13, across 1,500 square miles. It killed 453 people and injured 52,000 others. The flames reached along the North Shore as far as the French River, luckily missing the heart of Duluth. Though it was spared from the fires, Duluth was still greatly impacted by the flames and disease that followed.

While most of the community was fighting off the fires, others were fighting the influenza pandemic that peaked on October 15. The influenza pandemic took the lives of 327 Duluthians alone and about 12,000 Minnesotans. The pandemic put both the young and old at risk, and as a result, communities were forced to ban any parties, meetings, or funerals. People were required to stay at home for the safety of themselves and their neighbors. Students of the

Duluth Normal School were sent home and the school was closed, as was every other school in areas effected by the pandemic.

Helping the Hurting Community

October of 1918 was a time for the community to band together and offer support any way they knew how. That included Algot Nelson.

Nelson was a custodian at the Duluth Normal School. During the time of the fires, he "used his car to bring in several loads of fire victims for care and treatment in the Normal School gymnasiums." The Normal School was a safe haven from the fires.

Many area citizens found refuge in Duluth. The fire whipped through the land only a few miles south of the city. In Cloquet and Moose Lake, people found shelter wherever they could whether that was a plowed field, a well, or a body of water. Those desperate enough drove their cars into Moosehead Lake, looking for any sort of relief from the flames.

Feeding Those in Need

The people healthy enough to help did what they could, including Ruth Sloan, a domestic science instructor at the Duluth Normal School. Ruth supervised soup kitchens during the height of the pandemic with the aid of several "spirited" women. Together they "served soup, custards, and light puddings to some 250 to 300 patients a day in the influenza detention hospitals." The account of Ruth's kindness in *A Chronology of UMD Events: 1895-1984* is a testament to the help she gave to the community during the influenza crisis.

Repercussions of the Fire

The fire cost Minnesota $7.3 million, around $109 million today, in property destruction, and the pandemic took hundreds of thousands of lives all across the United States.

The Great Northern Railway was found responsible for the fire in 1920, but it wasn't until 1935 that victims from the fire saw any sort of financial justice. President Franklin D. Roosevelt signed a bill stating that victims should receive compensation for the damage done to their homes, buildings, and lives. Each community slowly rebuilt and said their goodbyes to those who were lost in both the fire and the influenza pandemic.

The Duluth Normal School banded together with the community and did what they could to help all those impacted by both natural disasters. By 1919, the Duluth Normal School was up and running but few forgot the aid the faculty and staff provided to the community.

by Ellie Mercil

___

The quoted sections in this story are from A Chronology of UMD Events: 1895-1984, *a document written by Clarence Anderson, University Relations Representative, and added to by other UMD staff members. The document and the banner photo are from the Archives and Special Collections, Kathryn A. Martin Library, University of Minnesota Duluth.*

7.

Schools in the Roaring 20s

From one-room schoolhouses to horse-drawn buses.

Helia Katherine Branwall (1897-1949) graduated from the Duluth Normal School in 1918. By 1923, Branwall was teaching third-grade at the Lincoln School in Esko, about 20 miles from Duluth.

Branwall's experience in Thompson Township presents an interesting perspective on society, the economy, and changes in education. It especially reflects on life in Duluth and the surrounding areas.

At the time Branwall graduated, the area was experiencing record growth. WWI was over and that brought the Roaring 20s, a decade in which America's economy grew by 42 percent. Job opportunities were growing too, as Duluth supported the birth of the automobile and airline industries with iron ore transport, increased traffic through Duluth's port, a new steel plant, and other industries.

Education was another area that was evolving. The U.S. educational system was undergoing massive change. Compulsory schooling laws enacted in 1900 meant that by 1910, 72 percent of American children attended school. Half of them attended one-room schools, although those schools were becoming fewer. By 1918, every state in the U.S. required students to complete elementary school.

The Transition from One-room to Single Grade Classrooms

The population of Esko was primarily made up by Finnish farming families. They built a one-room school in 1897 which closed in 1920. The children Branwall taught in her 1923 third-grade class may have had older brothers and sisters who attended that one-room school.

In the 1920s, residents, including Swedish and Norwegian immigrants, began to move into the area, and the township grew. Renowned 19th-century educator Horace Mann had advocated for the system of age grading, where students were assigned by age to different grades. The Thompson school district adopted the grade system for all their schools. Communities joined together to build the Lincoln School in 1920 and the Washington School in 1921.

Getting to School

Walking to school was no longer an option, so the children were transported to and from school in horse-drawn school buses. A picture from 1923 depicts a line of these buses outside of the Washington School in Esko. One can see the progress, as the horse-drawn buses are joined by four modern motorized vehicles.

Some of the horse-drawn school buses could transport up to 20 students. The children had to avoid frightening the animals, so they carefully got into the bus at the rear entrance.

The Teachers

The historical records don't show much about Branwall's life. What we do know from the archive and the photos is that she taught third grade at the Lincoln School, and she taught at the Washington School.

Branwall never taught in a one-room school. She is recorded in the Duluth Normal School records as graduating in 1918, and we have photos of her at the school in Esko in 1923 and 1936. We do know from the 1940 census that she lived in a boarding house near the two schools. She's listed as a "lodger" along with six women of various ages. One of the women who lived in the boarding house was Mabel Wongstedt, who graduated from the Duluth Normal School in 1925 and taught at the Washington School from 1935-36. Branwall's sister, Esther Elfina Branwell, also graduated from the Duluth Normal School and also taught in the Esko schools. The Esko Historical Society records state that Helia Branwall, the graduate from the Duluth Normal School, was "one of the longest-serving teachers" in the early Esko schools.

by Cheryl Reitan

_____

Banner photo: Helia Branwall and her third-grade class at the Lincoln School in Esko. Photo credits: Minnesota Historical Society and the Esko Historical Society. Much of the research for this story came from Esko's Corner, An Illustrated History of Esko and Thompson Township, *published by the Esko Historical Society.*

8.

May Fete

Welcoming the spring with song and dance.

"Dancing is as old as the human race, and it will endure as long as there are human emotions,"

May Fete photos from the UMD's Archives express magical paintings of nymphs and sprites dancing in the woods outside the Duluth State Teachers College (DSTC). Reality is not far off, as students performed dances and plays for the people of Duluth during several of the May Fete events.

The May Fete, or festival, was held every May, beginning in 1918 and ending with the last festival in 1940. During the 1930s, May Fete was run by Elizabeth Graybeal who was head of the Department of Physical Education. Miss Graybeal organized around 100 student participants and managed the entire event annually. Some U.S. colleges follow the old English tradition to this day, though some European and U.S. groups disapproved of the event because of its pre-Christian roots. May Fete at DSTC was viewed as an event that simply celebrated dance and springtime.

The event symbolized the renewal of life after the long winter season. It was like a right of passage, the start of a new beginning and the celebration of the completion of a milestone in someone's life.

The May Fete Experience

May Day marks the midpoint between the spring equinox and summer solstice, representing springtime, fertility, and light, so the event was always held outside and flowers were always present. Students would go out to collect hawthorn branches to decorate the DSTC grounds as well as their buildings. The festival would begin with the entrance of the May Queen and her court. The May Queen was voted by the entire female student body.

As the procession crossed the lawn, sounds of rustling skirts and the scent of lily-of-the-valley would drift over the audience. The May Queen would then receive her crown. The Master of Ceremonies introduced the Queen and her court as well as the performance for the event.

The pageant of music and dance was the festival's main attraction. Tickets were sold to Duluth citizens during some years; the archives show that once the tickets cost 10 to 25 cents, depending on the year. The college orchestra and Men's Glee club would accompany the dancers with song as they performed. Examples of different performances over the years would be the classic work of Modest Mussorgsky's The Great Gate of Kiev, several plays by William Shakespeare, and performances of Lewis Carroll's Alice's Adventures in Wonderland and Through the Looking Glass.

"Dancing is as old as the human race, and it will endure as long as there are human emotions," a statement read from the UMD Archives near the end of the May Fete tradition.

The May Pole

The group gathered again and the processions would wind its way to the Maypole, a painted pole, decorated with ribbons and flowers. The young women held long ribbons attached to the top of the pole and danced around the pole as they wove the ribbon into a pattern on the pole. The pole represented a living tree as the bright ribbons renewed its life and color after the winter stripped them away.

After a harsh Duluth winter, the May Fete was a breath of warm spring air to the community of Duluth and the student body of DSTC.

by Ellie Mercil

————

The banner photo is from the Archives and Special Collections, Kathryn A. Martin Library, University of Minnesota Duluth.

9.

Dawn of the Dawg

The Legend of the Bulldog: The Bark and the Bite.

The year was 1932. Football players ran down the field in a wave of Green and Gold. Not the Wisconsin Green Bay Packers, but intercollegiate athletes at Duluth State Teachers College (DSTC).

Before the UMD Bulldogs, athletes were known as the Green and Gold, or the Green Wave. They were also informally known as the Peds, short for Pedagogues, which is a word for teacher.

The Inspiration

In 1933, the spring football team officially gave their team a new name which first appeared in the Fortnightly Chronicle, the DSTC newsletter, on May 3. They called themselves the Bulldogs. It is said that the team name came from a football player, John "Jack"

O'Hehir. According to his teammates, his face resembled that of a bulldog.

The UMD Bulldog had a "ruff" journey for a while.

In 1956, some students had the Bulldog on a "tight leash". They wanted to change the mascot to another figure that better fitted Minnesota, with names like Falcons, Norsemen, Voyageurs, and Zeniths. Eventually, in 1957, a majority of students voted to keep the Bulldog name.

UMD's Bulldog

Twenty years went by before an unnamed costumed mascot made its first appearance at a basketball game against Concordia College in 1959. A name came easier for a living mascot. Semper Victorious, or Vicky, was UMD's real live bulldog mascot and in 1962 she made her first debut at the UMD-Michigan Tech hockey game.

Vicky proudly sported a maroon and gold sweater as she sauntered (and fell) on the ice rink. She was cared for by the members of Beta Phi Kappa at their fraternity house.

The original Bulldog costume was used at sporting events for many years. This Bulldog, a black-eyed, black-nosed, red-lipped mascot was first pictured in the UMD Statesman in October of 1962. The Chronicle yearbook had other photos, and the last Chronicle to picture this mascot was in the 1970 edition.

The Bulldog mascot in the 1980s

The second Bulldog costume made its debut in the 1980s. This plush, gray Bulldog known as "Killer" was popular from the mid-1970s to the early-1990s.

By the 1990s, the Department of Intercollegiate Athletics hosted a contest to rename the mascot, as some thought the name was too violent.

The debate circled the campus. Yale's Bulldog team has a mascot named "Handsome Dan" and Louisiana Tech's "Bulldog" football mascot is Champ, but there is no record of conversations about either school.

The most common memory is that students liked the name. "Champ" because it means a champion, a winner of a competition. With several conference and individual national championships under its belt, the student voters in the contest decided that the name, Champ, fit the bill.

"Champ" took the win as the mascots new name and the name was first announced at a UMD-Wisconsin hockey game on January 24, 1997.

Bulldog Logos

The Bulldog/Champ logo has taken many forms over the years, with the hand-drawn bulldog pictured in the banner photo (above) to dozens used in publications and events spanning decades.

The first official Bulldog logo was introduced during the 1969-1970 school year. The Bulldog was depicted in a series of logos, playing in several sports offered at UMD.

One year after UMD renamed the mascot, Champ, an updated Bulldog logo was created by UMD athletic department student intern Jesse Bodell.

Today, Champ's loveable, roly-poly, yet fierce features continue to inspire fans at sporting events. Children often line the aisles waiting for a High Five from Champ's furry hand.

From the Pedagogues in 1932 to the Champ and the Bulldogs in

2020, it's been a colorful and lively athletic history that still has fans cheering, "Go Dogs."

by Jessica Leung

—

The banner photo at the beginning of the chapter shows a student hanging green and gold streamers next to a bulldog painted on a wall for a 1940s Homecoming. The information and photographs in this article were researched and collected by UMD Archives student employee Tucker Nelson during the summer of 2019.

10.

Discovery in a New World

From Finland to the U.S., a student becomes a teacher.

When Olga Lakela gave the Cap and Gown Day address to UMD graduating seniors in 1958, she told them about the fields and meadows and the "purple heather and bluebell" near her childhood home in Kestila, Finland.

She spoke about her trip through Ellis Island with her parents on New Year's Day, 1906. It must have been a tremendous adventure, but it was only one of the many journeys she embarked on before she came to UMD as professor of biology in 1935.

Lakela left her second home in Biwabik, Minnesota, on her next journey in 1908. She traveled by train to Valparaiso, Indiana, where she invested all her savings in a comprehensive course in the English language and a two-year primary teaching program.

On her first day in class, she walked into a room filled with her Valparaiso classmates, all men.

Minot, North Dakota, came next. Again she traveled alone, this time to fulfill her two-year commitment, from 1910 to 1912, to teach in a primary school.

A Friend in Duluth

Her next stop was back in Minnesota. She met with E.W. Bohannon, president of the Duluth Normal School, in his office in Old Main. Bohannon became a friend who would guide her through five years of teaching in St Louis County and her own tuition-free higher education at Duluth Normal.

He must have seen the special spark in Lakela, because he stayed in touch with her as she earned degree after degree at the University of Minnesota. Her Bachelor of Science degree came in 1921 and her M.S. degree in 1924. She taught and became the biology department head at Minot North Dakota State Teachers College but was back at the University of Minnesota in 1930. A national Scientific Research Honor Society prize was bestowed in 1931 and finally, the Ph.D. in Botany and Zoology came in 1932. Her thesis was on the Genus Heuchera L. and that work played a major role in her later life's research.

Enchanted by Plants

Each day before class, from the earliest spring day until late fall, Lakela would rise at 5 a.m. and she search the hillside for plants to bring to class. On one of these excursions in 1938, she found something remarkable, a broadleaf grass. The plant, Poa Chaixii, was known in Europe and Asia but its discovery in North America is still credited to Lakela.

She never stopped preserving the items she collected. During her years in Duluth, Olga discovered two plants: Tiarella Cordiflora var. typica, a large-growing plant in Eastern woods of America, and Tiarella Cordiflora var. austrina, a heartleaf foamflower. She wrote about the rare Rubus chamaemorus, the Arctic cloudberry, and rediscovered Caltha natans, the floating marsh marigold, which hadn't been sighted since the early 1900s.

Amassing an Herbarium

Lakela gathered specimens by traveling to Lake, Cook, Aitkin, Itasca, Carlton, and Koochiching counties of Minnesota as well as points on the Canadian side of the border lakes. She hunted deep in the woods and fields of St. Louis County, and gathered more than 400 species on Duluth's Park Point alone.

She pressed and preserved these plants along with nearly 20,000 other plants and ferns, to build a substantial herbarium. Some of the specimens date as far back as 1846, with the majority of the collection from the 1940s. When she left UMD, the collection numbered 31,000, and in 2020, it contained more than 50,000 dried botanical specimens.

In the summer of 1939, Lakela left the shores of North America once again. UMD Professor Emeritus David Schimpf, one of the past directors of what is now called the Olga Lakela Herbarium, said she traveled to her birthplace in Kestila, Finland, and collected plants. "We have plant specimens in the Herbarium with the notation, 'Former Lakela Estate, 1939.' She must have traveled to the Arctic Ocean because she brought several plants from there as well." Schimpf calculates that Lakela traveled back to the States on an ocean liner right about the time Hitler was entering Poland at the start of WWII.

A Gift to Future Generations

When Lakela saw her UMD compulsory retirement in 1958 looming, she expanded her efforts toward the publication of a book, A Flora of Northeastern Minnesota. She praised UMD

Provost Raymond W. Darland for "his very great interest in the progress of this book and for his unsparing effort in securing means for its publication." Darland and many Duluthians made a valiant effort to raise the funds for the publication of the book in the 1950s, printing a brochure and garnering media coverage, but the funds fell short.

On December 28, 1965, more than seven years after she left UMD, Lakela's monumental reference book was printed by the University of Minnesota Press. It is still in print today. Described as a complete identification manual, it provides keys, descriptions, and distribution data for the ferns, fern allies, flowering plants, trees, shrubs, and herbs of the lake and forest country. Many of the 1,300 species it chronicles were previously unreported in Minnesota. It is illustrated with 110 drawings and 419 maps. The plants in it were found in a 9,000 square miles region, which includes the Superior National Forest and three continental river systems, a crossroad of plant migration.

The Legacy

Lakela held high honors at UMD. At the 1940 New York World's Fair, she was named among 650 foreign-born Americans honored on the "Wall of Fame" for distinguished achievement in her field. She was also listed in "Who's Who In America." In addition to her botanical work, she was an accomplished ornithologist. She taught, researched, lectured, and published on the topic.

After her retirement from UMD, Lakela continued her research at the University of South Florida in Tampa and helped to create a tropical Florida herbarium. Her discoveries there included a mint plant, Dicerandra immaculata, or Lakela's Mint. She continued to publish, right up until 1976, only four years before her death in 1980.

Olga left a permanent mark on UMD with the publication of her 1965 book and the establishment of the Olga Lakela Herbarium, which has continued to grow. She established a research fund to support the herbarium and the Biology Department as well. But perhaps the greatest legacy of all is the inspiration she gave to her colleagues, her students, and the community. She was an unrivaled role model, a generous and supportive leader, and a first-class researcher.

by Cheryl Reitan

———

The banner photo and research material came from the Archives and Special Collections, Kathryn A. Martin Library, University of Minnesota Duluth.

11.

Unparalleled Generosity

The Tweed family imparts their love of fine art.

George P. Tweed met the train at the Union Depot on Michigan Street in Duluth. The staff were waiting. They escorted Tweed to a cargo car where Tweed proceeded to open packages. The shipments came from New York City, Chicago, or Detroit, and the goods were transferred to a train in St. Paul to make the trip north. Tweed examined the contents of each package and sorted them into two piles: keep and return. Inside each package was a work of art.

George Tweed received the painting, "The Diggers" by Jean-Francois Millet, from railroad builder James J. Hill in a trade.

Tweed had a system. He received catalogues of art auctions and galleries via the postal service, and employed two art buyers to make purchases for him, on approval. When the trains arrived, he made his final choices, and returned the rest. One can see the selections Tweed made today in UMD's Tweed Museum of Art.

Rags to Riches

Tweed, born to Norwegian immigrants in rural Minnesota, made his fortune in the development of mines on Minnesota's Iron Range.

He held onto the fortune as a banker and financier. All through in the 1930s, between the world wars, European art was often sold to U.S. collectors and Tweed was among them.

Tweed's taste was called "unconventional," because he didn't follow popular trends. He purchased pieces from around the world and decades later, art appraisers discovered many pieces of "important work by significant artists" in the collection.

George made the purchases, but it was his wife, Alice, who hung the art in their home at 2309 East First Street in Duluth. That home, built by James Cotton in 1908, was an Italianate mansion, decorated with hand-carved stone, exotic woods, centuries-old Italian marbles, mosaics, and stained glass.

The Gallery

In 1941, the Tweeds moved. They donated the James Cotton Mansion to the Duluth State Teachers College (which became UMD in 1948). There, in the building now dubbed Tweed Hall, student art classes and art exhibitions were held. The carriage house was named the Tweed Annex and for a time, housed the ROTC offices.

The Tweeds' new home at 2631 East Seventh Street was well suited for an art gallery. Alice once again took over the decorating and the placement of the art. In one of the photographs UMD has of the Tweed Gallery, Jean-Francois Millet's painting, "The Diggers" is placed above the fireplace. That painting was a trade with the railroad builder James J. Hill and is arguably the most valuable piece in the collection.

The family, consisting of Alice, George, and their daughter Bernice, lived on the second and attic floors. Visitors were invited to visit the art collection one day a week. George Tweed died in 1946. The couple had amassed a collection of 300 paintings by 1950 when Alice Tweed donated the house and the collection to UMD.

On September 20, 1950, the Tweed Memorial Art Collection was formally opened with Alice Tweed, University of Minnesota President James Lewis Morrill, and other dignitaries in attendance. In 1955, the gallery had displayed more than 50 major exhibits to nearly 26,000 community groups, public school children, and college students. It remained in operation as a gallery until 1958.

A New Museum of Art

UMD needed a modern facility. Alice, now Alice Tweed Tuohy after her marriage in 1953, was ready to help. She and her daughter each made a substantial donation to the Tweed Museum of Art building fund, and in 1958 they were both in attendance at the dedication ceremonies.

The George P. Tweed Memorial Art Collection lives on. It's comprised of predominantly 19th century European and American art, including examples of the French Barbizon School and American Impressionist landscape paintings. Over the years, the Alice Tweed Tuohy Foundation has made significant contributions to the Tweed Museum of Art's renovation efforts and its acquisition funds.

Duluthian Generosity

Through the years, several important pieces of real estate were given to UMD.

Olcott Hall: In In 1940, Mrs. Dorothy Olcott Elsmith and Mrs. Elizabeth Olcott Ford donated the former Olcott home at 2316 East First Street to the Duluth State Teachers College (DSTC) as a center for musical study.

Darling Observatory: In 1944, longtime astronomer John Darling bequeathed his observatory at 910 West Third to the DSTC. It was used by the community and the campus for stargazing.

Nortondale Tract: In 1949, Regent Richard L. Griggs headed the citizen and civic group effort to purchase 160 acres of the Nortondale Tract to be used for UMD's new campus.

The Alworth Estate: In 1951, the estate of Royal D. and Mollie Alworth at 2627 E. Seventh Street was donated to UMD. Covering a full city block, it contained two large brick residences, a two-story brick garage and other buildings. The greenhouse was used by the UMD biology department.

Glensheen, the Historic Congdon Estate: In 1968, the estate of Chester and Clara Congdon at 3300 London Road, was given to UMD, which operates Glensheen as a historic house museum to this day. In 1979, the mansion opened to the public.

by Cheryl Reitan

The banner photo above is of the Tweed house taken in 1974.

12.

The Same Stars

From 1917 to 2020, thousands gaze up to capture the stars.

The Darling Observatory started Duluth's excitement for astronomy. For more than ninety years, Duluth and student interest in the stars have been propelled forward by a collection of telescopes, observatories, and one central planetarium.

John Henry Darling (see photo above) and the Darling Observatory began the story in 1917, but it took until the 1960s for UMD to bring a small telescope, and later a large planetarium, to campus.

The Darling Observatory

John Henry Darling was born in Michigan in 1847 and moved to

Duluth in 1884. He had a remarkable 40 year scientific career with the U.S. Army Corps of Engineers for forty years.

In 1903, he discovered magnetic variations over a portion of Lake Superior west of Devil's Island, which endangered navigation by drawing vessels from their courses. The resulting variations were mapped and published with diagrams and details of methods. These navigating aides were used by ship captains.

Darling retired in 1913 but never truly stopped working. He took up the hobby of stargazing, which grew into plans for a local observatory. There was no better place to build his observatory than Observation Park in downtown Duluth, named for having "one of the finest views in the city." With permission from the City of Duluth, construction was finished in 1917. At the completion, Darling had spent $11,000 on the observatory, including $3,500 for the telescope alone.

The observatory had a lecture room that seated up to 20 people. Darling opened the observatory to the public six or seven evenings a month to "allow people to view celestial objects and to educate them on astronomy." Darling's observatory contained a nine-inch refracting telescope made by William Gaertner & Co. The company was unable to obtain glass for the lens due to limited supplies during World War I. However, John A. Brashear, a Pennsylvania astronomer and instrument builder, had a nine-inch lens on hand. Darling designed some of the parts for his telescope himself.

After Darling's death in 1942, the observatory was willed to the City of Duluth with a trust fund of $20,000 to continue its operation. However, events transpired that changed the late Darling's wishes.

The Marshall W. Alworth Planetarium

In 1963, Provost Raymond W. Darland discussed with Marshall

W. Alworth the possibility of moving the Darling Observatory to campus. Instead, they chose to build a planetarium for both the students on campus and the Duluth public.

Mr. Marshall W. Alworth was the son of Marshall H. Alworth, who made a fortune in the mining, lumber, and real-estate industries of northern Minnesota. Marshall W. was a generous benefactor to UMD. He felt that a planetarium could be used day or night, summer or winter, could accommodate many people at a time, and would be an excellent teaching facility. The Marshall W. Alworth planetarium building was completed in 1967.

Darling Revisited

For many years, UMD considered taking over the Darling Observatory, but no purchase was agreed on. Instead of thriving, as Darling hoped, poor management, low public interest, and vandalism to the dome resulted in the building being dismantled in 1972.

The dome ended up in a junkyard, which was once an area of Canal Park. Luckily, the telescope was taken apart and laid to rest in the tunnel beneath UMD.

In 1967, Donald Jackson, the Planetarium Director, worked on purchasing several telescopes for university use. In the 1980s, Eric Norland, a UMD art major, suggested to Jackson that the Darling telescope should be put on exhibit in the planetarium lobby, which at the time was completely open and empty. Liking the idea, Jackson pulled some strings and the telescope found a good home on permanent display, still standing there to this day, with its eye up to the stars.

Campus Observatory

The dream for Marshall W. Alworth Hall to be able to hold an astronomical observatory on its roof with a 16 inch Cassegrain telescope built by Group 128 installed soon after. The dream did not last long as the dome and telescope were removed in 1985 due to poor performance.

Fortunately, the dome was not discarded. It was given to a supporter of UMD's Physics & Astronomy Department Glenn Langhorst, pictured to the right, who has maintained and used the dome on his private property. Langhorst has recently returned the dome to UMD. Fundraising efforts are underway to give new life to the original dome. The plan is to reinstall the dome on the roof of Marshall W. Alworth Hall. It will also house a new 17-inch Planewave telescope.

To discuss a contribution to the UMD Observatory, please contact Carrie Sutherland, senior development officer, at 218-726-6984 or csutherl@d.umn.edu.

by Ellie Mercil

—

The banner photo of the Darland Observatory at 910 West Third Street came from the Archives and Special Collections, Kathryn A. Martin Library, University of Minnesota Duluth.

13.

John Hatten: 70 Years as a Bulldog

From DSTC grade school to UMD graduate school dean.

As a boy, John Hatten attended the Laboratory School, a small elementary school operated by the Duluth State Teachers College (DSTC). He remembers coming to his fourth-grade classroom in 1947 and finding it filled with items he had never seen before. The items came from Robert James Vessel, Hatten's student teacher, who had served in the U.S. Marine Corps in WWII.

"He brought all sorts of things," such as tea sets, eating utensils, and clothing, says Hatten.

Vessel spent time with the students, explaining about each of the "artifacts from Japan." There were woven scrolls, kimonos, and wooden boxes. Vessel told the students how customs and culture differ around the world.

Hatten described Mr. Vessel as being kind. Years later, when Vessel was honored for his generosity to UMD, Hatten and Vessel corresponded by mail. In fact, Hatten sent a copy of the photograph of the classroom to Vessel.

Young Classmates

Many of the Lab School students stayed in touch. Some were in the same class at East High School, and some met up again in college at UMD. Hatten can name some of the students in the photo, but not all. He is the "shortest student in the class," third from the right.

"The fourth student from the left in the photo is Chauncey Wales Riggs," says Hatten. "He taught me to play tennis when I was a little kid and later we went to East High School together."

"The third guy from the left is Dick Fox and Nancy Peterson (next to Hatten) was in my class and she was very athletically skilled." Nancy's father, Lloyd William Peterson, was the football coach and later served as the UMD basketball coach, wrestling coach, and athletic director.

The girl standing to the left of the dark patterned kimono is Wynetka Ann King. "Her father [John E. King] became provost of the university." King was a teacher at DSTC and became UMD provost from 1950-53.

Adventures in the 1940s

Hatten adored his older brother, Bob, and the two of them had many adventures. "One night, Bob and I took a rake and pulled down the fire escape," Hatten says. It was a metal ladder on the side of the Laboratory School. "We climbed as high as we could." But when their mother came looking for them, she saw them on the top of the building. They got in trouble, and Hatten told his mother he would never do it again. "And I never did."

Going to school was also an adventure. "There was a great big Saint Bernard named Marlow, who came to school with one of the older students," says Hatten. "He was loved by the whole school. At the first recess, whenever you got out, the first thing you had to do was hug Marlow."

It seems like an idyllic setting. "There were owls around," says Hatten, "Lot's of owls, and there was a river [Oregon Creek] that went under and around Old Main and that was a playing spot."

Hatten has a story about the "UMD Upper Campus" before it was operational. He tells about stealing lumber from the Science Building construction site with another young boy. They took the lumber a few blocks down the hill into a woods in order to build a fort. Later that night they slipped out of bed and met each other on the street. Full of remorse, and possibly daunted by the prospect of sawing and nailing the heavy boards, they took them all back.

Familiar Faces

The list of prominent DSTC faculty Hatten saw in the halls is lengthy. After he attended Duluth East High School, he attended UMD and saw many familiar (and renowned) faces on campus.

There was botany faculty member Olga Lakela (Lakela Herbarium), industrial education faculty Gordon Voss and Frank Kovach (Voss Kovach Hall), and Ray Darland (Darland Administration Building) who arrived in 1949 as botany professor. Other UMD professors included Theron Odelaug, James McClear, Maude L. Lindquist, and Gerhard von Glahn.

The Academic Path

Hatten received a B.S. from UMD in 1959, an M.A. from Purdue University in 1961, and his Ph.D. in 1965 from the University of Wisconsin-Madison. Prior to the start of his teaching career at UMD, he was a public school speech-language pathologist at

Downers Grove Public Schools, and an assistant professor of speech pathology at Northern Michigan University. As a faculty member at UMD beginning in 1967, the courses he taught included phonetics, communication disorders, and language disorders.

His career brought him classes, students, publications, and presentations. He took on the role of associate dean of the graduate school and through it all, touched many lives.

While he and his wife Pequetti divide their time between Edina, Minnesota, California, and Arizona, he has never forgotten the experiences he had in Duluth and he keeps UMD in his thoughts.

by Cheryl Reitan

—

The banner photo is from the collection of John Hatten. A copy of the photo is located in the Archives and Special Collections, Kathryn A. Martin Library, University of Minnesota Duluth.

14.

"Bulldogma" Reigns at Post-War UMD

What a year! 1947-48 brings exploration, exams, and events.

When World War II ended, the United States experienced phenomenal economic growth, and veterans spilled into colleges. By 1946-47, there were so many military veterans in class at the University of Minnesota in Minneapolis, students had to sit on the window sills because there weren't enough chairs.

During this time, the citizens of Duluth rallied to win the long-time struggle to transform the Duluth State Teachers College (DSTC) into a university with a full university curriculum. They wanted Duluth to join the University of Minnesota. Duluthian Richard Griggs and Minnesota Representative A.B. Anderson were just two of the people who fought a battle for legislative and regent approval for the plan. They finally succeeded during the last minutes of the 1947 legislative session.

By the fall of 1947, the campus on the hillside experienced its first year with its new name, the University of Minnesota – Duluth Branch. The G.I. Bill offered grants to help pay for college tuition, and that, along with the euphoria that continued to sweep over the country at war's end, meant full classrooms in Duluth. And so the year began...

A Homecoming for the Heart

Many already know of a man named Dan Devine; a man who had a legendary career as a football player, and coach.

He coached football at Arizona State University and the University of Missouri before taking on championship years with the Green Bay Packers and the University of Notre Dame football teams.

Many don't know that Devine got his start in Duluth. After graduating from Proctor High School and serving in the Air Force during WWII, he was recruited to play basketball at the Duluth State Teachers College (DSTC). He majored in history. Devine's exploits in college athletics were chronicled in the Statesman student newspaper in a column entitled "Bulldogma," written by student George McNamara.

There was another addition to Devine's life. He met a young woman, his college classmate, named JoAnne Brookhart. Now Devine had seen the world and he had a certain confidence in his decisions, on and off the field. So when he proposed to JoAnne, they didn't waste time. By the start of their senior year, they were married.

According to 1955 UMD alumnus Ben Korgan, with Devine as the starting quarterback, "the team came alive." By the fall of 1947, Dan was captain of the football team and president of the senior class. When the time came for the student body to vote for homecoming queen, they chose JoAnne Devine. And UMD won the homecoming game, too.

A Homecoming Flight

William "Bill" Bianco, like so many of his classmates, fit a service career into his college career. He enrolled in Duluth State Teachers College after graduation from Denfeld in June 1947 and completed two years at UMD prior to his service in the Navy.

As the story goes... Bianco and his friend, Paul Davidson, were pilots. Davidson was a pilot in WWII, and they both flew Piper Cub planes out of the Duluth airport. In fall 1947, their friend, Kathleen "Kitty" Bocklund, a Denfeld High School classmate, was running for homecoming queen. Kitty's election committee printed postcard-sized fliers that said "Kitty for Queen." In a 2002 interview with UMD, Bianco said, "Near the date of homecoming, Paul came flying with me... and we flew low over the campus, at about 500 feet, and Paul opened the door and dumped the box."

Things didn't go as planned... in many ways. The cards were picked up by the wind and flew all over the neighborhood. Bianco and Davidson were grounded for weeks for flying too close to the ground. Kitty did get enough votes to be part of the homecoming court, though, so all was not lost.

Adventures didn't end for Bianco. After graduating, he got married and was called back into service in the Korean conflict. He attended officers candidate school and served in the Marines before leaving active duty. He became an assistant vice president of a bank in Rochester, Minnesota, and later moved to Bismarck, North Dakota, where he was successful in business for 30 years until his retirement.

Campus Life

The year broke records. The school started with nearly 1,500 students, a 300 percent increase from the year before. There were so many new students that the dormitories couldn't hold them all, so Duluthians offered to take students into their homes.

Many new faculty arrived at UMD in 1947, including Richard Sielaff, who taught business administration. The students didn't know it then, but Sielaff would go on to UMD's School of Business and Economics, which was created in 1974.

With a growing student body, the year was full of events. Music lovers had the opportunity to hear Marian Anderson sing at the Duluth Armory. Anderson was considered the world's greatest living contralto, and she presented a program of classics, operatic arias, and spirituals. She also made civil rights history in 1939. After the Daughters of the American Revolution refused permission for Anderson to sing in Constitution Hall in Washington, DC, First Lady Eleanor Roosevelt and President Franklin D. Roosevelt invited her to sing at the Lincoln Memorial in the capital. Anderson sang before an integrated crowd of more than 75,000 people and a radio audience in the millions.

Back on campus, band, choir, orchestra, and theatrical shows were performed by the students. There was even a modern dance recital and a Norwegian art exhibit.

No one could disagree, UMD arrived in Minnesota with excitement and fanfare.

by Cheryl Reitan

Banner photo above: Dan Devine presents his wife JoAnne Brookhart Devine with flowers during UMD's 1947 Homecoming ceremonies.

15.

Sno Week's Chill and Cheer

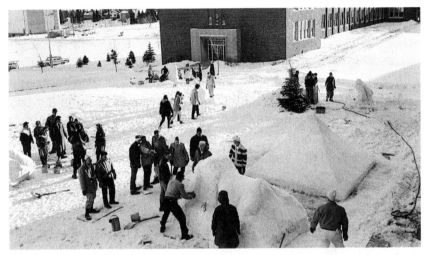

Winter festivities add warmth during Duluth's harshest season.

Sno Week was a week-long celebration at UMD, from its inception in 1950 until the last Sno Week dance in 1972. Every year brought a different set of events. Over the two-plus decades, UMD presented nearly every winter activity under the sun, and most of the celebrations ended with a large, semi-formal dance called Sno Ball.

Some years, students went dashing through the snow... literally. They called the series of athletic activities a Sno Trek, and one of the events was a 50-yard-dash through deep snow. According to the Statesman, in addition to the race, the 1953 Sno Trek included "cross country skiing, speed skating, snowshoeing, and a sleigh pull across the broomball rink."

Every Sno Queen had her king. For many years, the Sno King was decided by the best beard. In 1954, the contest description read, "The chin foliage, which is requested to be cultivated by all male students on campus, started its growth on the first of February." That same year, the King was decided after the square dance and the winner was given a $10 prize and the honor of crowning the Sno Queen. According to the Statesman, "It took four judges to choose the longest and fullest beard grown by the male member of UMD."

Students loved a Ski Trip. In 1954, UMD students went to Lutsen Ski resort to kick off Sno Week. For many years, the ski trip started with a ride on a Greyhound bus, nicknamed the "sno-caravan," picking students up and heading up to Lutsen. The midnight bus ride home became commonly known as the "dawn yawn." In 1957, they went to Sawtooth Mountain in Grand Marais, and in 1958, the ski trip was held at Mount Telemark in Cable, Wisconsin.

For one year, in 1958, Sno Week changed its name to Schneefest, (schnee means snow in German), and that change garnered the attention of the German populations in both Minnesota and Wisconsin. The events included, "a sleigh ride, ski trip, polka dance, sled dog races, and a snow sculpture." The week was described as full of "fun, frolic and pulchritude" (which means desirability). The '58 ski trip cost only $8.50, around $75 today. Students received "transportation to and from Cable, two meals while there, and [their] tow fees for the day."

Schneefest drew national attention in 1958. Fox-Moveitone heard about UMD's annual event and arranged to come to Duluth in early March to film UMD students. Tom McMorrow, a sports anchor for Fox-Movietone at the time, visited campus and was charmed by the "birches and pines" on the lower campus. McMorrow, who called the feature, "Winter fun on the American campus," asked for all available UMD students to be part of the filming, which included a sled dog race, a broomball game, skating, and ski-jouring.

The Snow Sculpture contests that took place in front of Kirby Student Center were quite popular and drew many students out into the deep freeze every year. Sculpting was done one day and judging was done the next, allowing the snow to freeze overnight. Some of the more elaborate sculptures included a large snow train, a snow sphinx, and a perfect snow pyramid.

The final UMD Sno Week activity was held in the Bullpub (now the Rafters) in 1972. The eight-piece show band was named Package, and it was accompanied by two "go-go" girls.

by Ellie Mercil

——

The banner photo and quotes in this story are from the Archives and Special Collections, Kathryn A. Martin Library, University of Minnesota Duluth.

16.

Odlaug's Plankton Research

Students conduct Great Lakes research on ore boats.

Archie J. Vomachka was a biology student at UMD in the late 1960s, and he has vivid memories of an unusual research project at UMD. One of his professors, Theron O. Odlaug, received funding for a three-year baseline study of plankton in Lake Superior, Lake Michigan, and Lake Huron.

Somehow, Odlaug had made arrangements with the United States Steel's Pittsburgh Steamship Company and the Hanna Furnace Corporation Steamship Company to allow UMD to drag equipment behind ore carriers on 45 voyages, during three summers: 1967, 1968, and 1969.

It was a tremendous adventure for the college students. Archie, his brother Jon Vomachka, and others, collected plankton data on the long voyages. Their friend and classmate, Ed Bersu stayed dockside to analyze the samples. They all remember joining the ore boat crew to load the massive CPR (continuous plankton recorder) up on the deck and then mount it to the back of the ship.

On Board

Archie recalls a fateful trip. "We were coming back to Duluth, when we heard a huge boom" he says. "The carrier kept plowing along, but we knew something was wrong." When they got to the back of the ship, they could see that the stainless steel cable had snapped. "I can't imagine what the recorder caught on, but it had to be massive and heavy."

Jon recalls a similar mishap, but the consequences were more severe. His team lost a plankton recorder too, but it was at the beginning of the trip, before any specimens had been gathered.

"We left Taconite Harbor in the middle of the night," Jon says. "Two of us were lowering the recorder into the water and the winch suddenly jammed. The winch was half the size of a refrigerator with a crank on each side." Jon and his partner thought the brake shoe was stuck so they hammered on it in order to break it free. They were successful in loosening it, too successful. "We heard the recorder going all the way down, 1000 feet, to the bottom of the lake."

Twice, Archie traveled on the Cason J. Callaway across Lake Superior, through the Soo Locks, at Sault Ste Marie, into Lake Michigan, and back. Once the ship stopped in Gary and the other time in Hammond, Indiana. Jon went on too many trips to count. He went out every year for the three years of the study. He traveled on Lake Superior, Michigan, and Huron, for the study and even went to Lake Erie, when the ship had an extra stop to make.

The students were treated well. "We ate meals at the captain's table, and spent a fair amount of time in the wheelhouse," Archie says. Day and night they collected samples, pulling in specimens caught in the fine silk screen mesh inside the plankton recorder.

Back in Minnesota

Ed Bersu traveled to the ore boats with other students and assistants, but he never took a long voyage. He remembers going to the Cason J. Callaway. "I was with Mike Adess, UM-Twin Cities doctoral student, and we had to get the plankton recorder to the dock in Two Harbors." There were other students from the University of Minnesota School of Public Health doing plankton research for Odlaug's study: William Parkos, Robert Nelson, and Art Charbonneau.

Professors Theron O. Odlaug and Theodore A. Olson reviewed the routes the plankton recorder would cover.

Most of the time, Ed joined other student workers to analyze the data back in the Limnology Lab. The 45 voyages yielded a great amount of plankton life to be recorded.

Odlaug's research study set out to do something never done before. They were the first to demonstrate the usefulness of the continuous plankton recorder to a freshwater research program. They also obtained baseline information about water quality based on an analysis of zooplankton occurrence and distribution in the Great Lakes.

How It Started

Beginning in the mid-50s, Odlaug, UMD professor of biology, was the co-director of a University of Minnesota program that provided training and research experience in aquatic biology for teachers, graduate students, and public health personnel. Odlaug, who studied zooplankton, set up the UMD Limnological Research Center on London Road.

In the early 1960s the research vessels, the Oneota, an older wood-hulled boat, and the SS Jacobs, a newer steel-hulled vessel were used for research. They were docked at Knife River, Minnesota. Jon remembers helping graduate students conduct summer research studies by diving off the boats for samples.

The Ecology of the Second Trophic Levels Study

The Great Lakes plankton study started in 1966, when Odlaug's program received funding to purchase four CPRs (continuous plankton recorders), at that time, a novel sampling device. He enlisted the steamship companies, collaborated with other universities, set up a research lab, and hired students.

The experiment started with readings from the Research Vessels Oneota and Jacobs, shown here off Knife Island, near Knife River, Minnesota, in Lake Superior.

Three ore carriers hosted the scientists; the S.S. Cason J. Callaway, S.S. Sewell Avery, and the S.S. Ernest T. Weir. Odlaug appreciated the seamen. He publicly thanked the crews, "for their willing hand at the winch and the long periods of 'yarning' in the blacked-out wheelhouse, which made the long nights easier."

The teams collected a continuous record of the microscopic plants and animals in three of the Great Lakes from 1965-1969. Odlaug, along with Theodore A. Olson and Wayland R. Swain, compiled their findings in a 1970 study, "The ecology of the second trophic levels in Lake Superior, Michigan, and Huron."

The Impact on the Students

Archie Vomachka, Edward Bersu, and Jon Vomachka, the UMD students who worked with Dr. Odlaug on the plankton study, speak highly of the experience. The positive environment in the lab and the support of the professors made a lasting impression on the students.

Jon says, "It was a formative experience; it changed my life." When he first started working on the project, he was more enamored with carpentry than academia. That changed as he was able to merge his (by all accounts) remarkable mechanical skill with Dr. Odlaug's research requirements. Jon received his bachelor's and master's degree in biology at UMD and went on to teach public school science for 13 years and serve as a principal for 21 years.

Archie's success was stellar as well. From the Ph.D. in Zoology at Michigan State all the way to founding dean of the College of Health Sciences at Arcadia University, in Pennsylvania, Archie's accomplishments didn't stop. He has dozens of publications and scores of scholarships, awards, honors, and grants to his name. And still, after all these decades, he remembers Dr. Odlaug for inspiring a career in the life sciences.

Ed's accomplishments speak for themselves: Ph.D. from the University of Wisconsin-Madison, and a position as an expert on gross human anatomy and anatomical variations, as well as human embryology for the University of Wisconsin-Madison Medical School. Ed, too recalls Dr. Odlaug. "I remember thinking, if I could be as good of a teacher as any of my professors at UMD, I would be a success."

by Cheryl Reitan

_____

The banner photo at the beginning of the chapter was provided by Archie Vomachka. He is shown here on the S.S. Cason J. Callaway at the Mackinac Bridge.

17.

A Lifetime of Music

Ann Carlson Anderson: teacher, leader, and performer.

It is 1956. The crisp violin notes reverberate in a basement room of Olcott Hall. Deep inside the Georgian mansion, music student Ann Carlson is practicing for the UMD orchestra. The notes strike against the plaster walls. The room, formerly used to store coal that heated the huge house, provides a sound barrier between Ann and the rest of the world.

The practice rooms, two floors above, have gleaming wood floors, carved woodwork, and huge windows that look out on Lake Superior and one of Duluth's opulent neighborhoods. The rooms are filled with other music students, all practicing. But on this day, Ann can't practice there. She needs solitude. The orchestral piece she is working on is difficult, and she needs to concentrate.

After those moments as a student at UMD, Ann went on to a long career. Her story, both before and after her time in the coal room, is rare and remarkable indeed.

The Journey

Life wasn't always easy. Ann grew up in Austin, Minnesota, where she proved to be extremely talented in music and a good student as well. She was named the high school salutatorian and received partial scholarships to Carlton and St. Olaf colleges. But the cost of the rest of tuition and living expenses at those colleges were still too much for her family to support.

By the end of her senior year, the prospects for college looked bleak. But Ann's role in the Austin High School Orchestra and her performance at the Big 9 Festival changed everything.

Southern Minnesota had a special yearly event called the Big 9 Festival. It had its first year in 1927 and is still the oldest music festival of its kind in the United States. To this day, it showcases select high school ensembles in southern Minnesota. Every band, orchestra, and choir shows up from area schools that include Albert Lea, Austin, Faribault, Mankato, Northfield, Red Wing, Rochester, and Winona.

It was spring 1953. "I was at a practice for the Big 9," Ann says. "Students from all the schools made up the orchestra; and we had a guest conductor, Herman Hertz from the Duluth Symphony." During the practice, all of the orchestra conductors from all of the schools were walking between the students. "I didn't really know what was going on but when the piece was over, I had been named the concertmaster."

That concert led to another opportunity; she was invited to apply to UMD. Unknown to Ann, developments were falling into place. Mr. Hertz returned to Duluth and met with Gus Andreson, who was on the board of the Duluth Symphony. Hertz also met with the

UMD music faculty band conductor Pete Magnell. Gus Andreson made Ann an offer. In exchange for Ann's full tuition as a violin major, Ann would perform as a student member with the Duluth Symphony.

First Years in Duluth

Ann began attending UMD in 1953 on the full-ride scholarship. She played piano and performed in the UMD orchestra as a gifted violinist. She also played clarinet in the band, but she admits, "I wasn't very good at the clarinet."

UMD provided Ann with an education, musical experience in the orchestra and the band, and life experiences like eating eyeballs and worms. Well… that's a story.

Piano teacher E. Ruth Van Appledorn was Ann's favorite. Miss Appledorn was the faculty advisor for a music club known as the Buckhorns, and they had a special initiation for new members.

Ann's initiation involved blindfolds, eyeballs (peeled grapes), and rattlesnake meat. The freshmen were blindfolded and instructed to eat or touch something. Ann did neither. She ran away screaming, dodging her slimy fate, and sending the rest of the group into unstoppable laughter.

Olcott Hall, Tweed Hall, and the Fine Arts

Classes and music practice filled Ann's days. Most of Ann's classes were at the lower campus. Only five buildings were on the upper campus at the time: the Science Building, Athletic Building, Kirby Student Center, ROTC, and the Vermilion Hall residence, although more construction was on the way.

The music students spent lots of time in opulent mansions. "Olcott Hall was the music center," says Ann. Olcott Hall, at 2316 E. First Street, is noted for being Duluth's most impressive example of Georgian architecture, and it was a treat for Ann and her classmates to spend time there. The home was donated to the Duluth State Teachers College (DSTC) in 1939 and sold in 1958.

Across the street, at 2309 E. First Street, was Tweed Hall, the location of UMD's Arts and Humanities Department. "The art students had their classes there, and there was a gallery for art exhibitions too," Ann says.

Ann spent many days in Tweed Hall's carriage house, or as she calls it, "the garage." That's where the orchestra practiced. Recitals were held in the living room.

Tweed Hall was a grand mansion for those fortunate students. It was built in 1908 by Joseph Cotton, a lawyer, and sold to George P. and Alice Tweed. The Tweed family donated the Italian Renaissance mansion to the DSTC in 1941.

The two halls, along with the Old Main auditorium, offered lots of places for students to perform concerts, musicals, and operas.

Out in the World

After college, Ann married and disaster struck. Her husband, Don Anderson, suffered an incurable brain injury and tragically died.

Ann turned to music for solace. She threw herself into her work and took her first professional position as a violinist with the New Orleans Symphony. She went on to stints with the Indianapolis Symphony, the Metropolitan Opera National Co., the Aspen Festival Orchestra, and the American Arts String Quartet.

In 1968, Ann was giving concerts with the American Arts String Quartet based in Green Bay, Wisconsin. They had been recently flown to Duluth twice to perform with the Duluth Symphony, but one day, Ann received a different kind of call. It was from UMD. There was an opening for a music teacher, and UMD wanted her to apply.

Ann returned to UMD to teach the musical arts. "It felt like home," Ann said. "I had so many friends here, and the students were so eager to learn." More than ever, the days were busy with class, private lessons, and concerts.

During this time, Ann became one third of a musical ensemble with Pat LaLiberte, who played the piano. Sometimes Eugenia "Jeanie" Slezak, who played the cello, joined them, especially when they traveled to high schools across Northern Minnesota. They performed and encouraged students to attend UMD after graduation.

Among the many awards Ann has received over the years is the 1992 Master Teacher Award from the Minnesota American String Teachers Association and the honor of serving as an outreach artist by the St. Louis County Heritage and Arts Center. In 2012, Ann was inducted into the School of Fine Arts' Society of Prometheans. This honor recognizes individuals who have demonstrated passion, commitment, and talent to achieve the highest levels of excellence in their art and profession.

Now, Ann is happily retired. She drives around Duluth to events nearly every day and continues to play music. Every year, her scholarship, the Ann Carlson Anderson Symphonic String Scholarship, is presented to a UMD student. And she still performs in the Duluth Superior Symphony Orchestra and holds the title of Associate Concertmaster Emeritus.

"Coming back to UMD was one of my best decisions," she says.

by Cheryl Reitan

———

The banner photo at the beginning of the chapter is of Ann Anderson at a UMD orchestra practice in 1969.

18.

Swedes at the Tweed

Traditional Swedish art pushes its way into modernity.

On a brisk April day in 1961, the Tweed Art Gallery formally opened a display of Swedish art, which included a "194-piece exhibit of Swedish glass, crystal, woven products, and ceramics." The huge crowd of more than 1,000 people who joined the celebration was a testament to the popularity of Scandinavian design at the time and a reflection of the large population of people of Scandinavian descent in Minnesota.

The exhibit was put together by Orazio Fumagalli, the Tweed's associate director, along with first secretary of the Swedish embassy in Washington, Gunnar N. Lonaeus, and Swedish Consul General in Minneapolis, Gösta af Petersens.

Collections and pieces were borrowed for the exhibition from the Gustavsberg factory, the Rörstrand factory, and other Swedish firms. The exhibit was designed by Fumagalli, a renowned sculptor, who went on to have a long career as an artist and professor.

To honor the exhibit's grand opening, Swedish Prime Minister Tage Erlander, his wife, Aina Anderson Erlander, and the Swedish Ambassador to the U.S., Gunnar Jarring, paid a special visit to Duluth after meeting with President Kennedy in Washington, D.C. Their stop in Duluth marked the beginning of a quick tour around America.

Prime Minister Erlander was delighted by his visit to Duluth and found many touches of home among its hills. He said, "You have the forests and the inland lakes and rivers around you. You have iron ore. And you have a large body of water comparable to the Baltic Sea." Provost Raymond W. Darland and Prime Minister Erlander opened the exhibit. Erlander commented, "It is a great personal satisfaction to me to be present when Sweden is presenting an art exhibit in a city such as Duluth." He called Duluth, "a city with an open mind and a keen appreciation of art."

One notable designer for some of the pieces was Wilhelm Kage of the Gustavsberg factory, which is situated on the island of Värmdö in Sweden's Stockholm archipelago. Kage was well known for being one of the first pioneers of 'Swedish Modern.' "His heavy, powerful forms and deep glowing glazes are unmistakably typical of this grand old man among the Swedish ceramicists," Lonaeus wrote when he described the crafts of Sweden. Another memorable collection was the one-of-a-kind stoneware pieces by Carl-Harry Stålhane, who was chief of design at the Rörstrand factory, which at the time, was located on Kungsholmen Island in Stockholm. Stig Lindberg, the artistic leader of the Gustavsberg factory, and many others, had their pieces displayed at the Tweed.

The pieces to the left reflect the Scandinavian design movement, characterized by simplicity, minimalism, and functionality that flourished in the 1950s. Work by Wilhelm Kage of the Gustavsberg factory is at the far left, a collection of mid-century Swedish art glass is in the center, and on the right is work by Stig Lindberg of the Gustavsberg factory. These pieces reflect another influential design show named Design in Scandinavia, which traveled to 24 museums throughout the U.S. and Canada from 1954-57.

Lonaeus described the Tweed exhibition with these words, "Due to Sweden's comparatively late industrialization, the folk art tradition, with its emphasis on the functional simplicity and gay decorative pattern, prevailed longer in Sweden than in many other countries, and was given a new lease on life through the craft movement."

The exhibit was welcomed by a huge crowd at the opening and even more visitors throughout its stay at the Tweed.

by Ellie Mercil

The banner photo and quoted sections of this story are from the collection of the Tweed Museum of Art. Special thanks to Karissa White Isaacs, associate curator, for helping find the original photos and documents.

19.

UMD's Own Harry Oden

Basketball champion, scholarship sponsor, lifetime humanitarian

It was 1963. The buzzer went off at the end of an eventful basketball game in the Physical Education Building gym. Harry Oden, a senior, was captain and UMD's Most Valuable Player. He was on the All-Conference first team and the University of Minnesota system's first black basketball captain. He gazed into the stands.

He took a long look at a sea of faces. "They were all faces that didn't look like me," he says. Oden, with more baskets already in that season than any other player, won the game for the Bulldogs. To his right, his teammates crowded together.

"In my four years at UMD, I was never invited to go out and

celebrate," he says. "I never knew a cheerleader's name, and was never congratulated after a game by any one of the cheerleaders." That night, he went back to his dorm to study.

During those years, Oden felt alone for more reasons than the exclusion of his classmates and teammates. "I was in Duluth for three weeks before I saw another black face," he says. Duluth was much different from his hometown in Milwaukee, where he was surrounded by a black community. In Duluth and other places, while traveling for games, he was refused service at the movies, restaurants, and hotels. Oden went through long years dealing with the racism and hatred that came with being a black man in the 1960s. Because of the basketball schedule, he spent years of Thanksgivings, Christmases, New Year's Eves, and Easters, alone. Only once did one of his teammates offer to bring Harry to his home.

One day in his sophomore year, Oden packed up to leave Duluth for good. He even made it downtown to the bus station with his suitcase before he turned back. Getting a college education was too important to him, and there were people who cared. "Norm Olson, the basketball coach, supported me." Oden also mentions Lloyd Peterson, the athletic director, and Jim Malosky, the football coach, who encouraged him. "But the main reason I turned around was because of something I told my father before he passed away," Oden says. "I promised my father that I would go as far as I could in school."

As Oden attended UMD, national civil rights struggles loomed. North Carolina saw violent protests over "whites only" lunch counters. The University of Alabama blocked black students from registering. At the March on Washington for Jobs and Freedom, Martin Luther King gave his "I Have A Dream" speech.

The summer after Oden's senior year, he was visiting his grandparents in Alabama when a bomb at Birmingham's 16th Street Baptist Church killed four young black girls. Oden traveled to Birmingham that same Sunday. "I wanted to see if I could help in some way." It's no wonder Oden calls these years, "Some of the toughest years of my life."

Civil rights had become personal. Earlier in Oden's senior year, no Duluth school would give him an opportunity to do his student teaching. It was a low spot in Oden's career. Lloyd Peterson, the athletic director, and Coach Norm Olson came to the rescue. They found Oden a position at Morgan Park High School. He student taught under Graydon Stromme, a history teacher, Morgan Park's basketball coach, a basketball player, and an avid UMD basketball fan.

Oden's professors were also a refuge. "I had some great instructors," Oden says. "They treated me fairly." Oden received support from teachers in his major. "History prof Arthur Larsen was my best and favorite instructor and Dr. James McClear, another history prof, taught me so much."

With this support from faculty and staff, Oden left UMD with an undergraduate degree in education in 1964 and a master's in history and education administration in 1980.

Recruitment

Oden's effort to bring basketball players to UMD started early. When he was just a junior, he started driving high school basketball players up to Duluth from Milwaukee to check out UMD. That pride in UMD and confidence in the UMD faculty and staff never wavered.

After he received his degree in education administration, his career in the Milwaukee Public Schools began. It lasted for 35 years. As a high school teacher at first, and later as a high school principal, he dedicated his life to community service.

He continued with the road trips to Duluth. He piled students into his car and drove them to UMD to show students what the campus had to offer. He often paid for hotels, meals, and other student expenses.

When Oden's car became too small, he worked with other Milwaukee educators to bring students from all over the area by the busload on recruitment trips to UMD. So deep was his commitment, on occasion, he actually paid the shortfall in an incoming UMD student's tuition.

Run for Excellence

Oden's generosity did not go unnoticed. In 1994, UMD's African American Student Services Coordinator Ken Foxworth took a bold step.

Foxworth finished a Run For Excellence, a 154-mile run from St. Paul to Duluth. Foxworth started at the St. Paul Capitol and ended at Duluth's City Hall. That's where Foxworth brought Harry Oden to the stage and announced that the $56,000 raised would become the Harry Oden Scholarship for Minority Students and Students with Disabilities. The next year, in 1995, Harry ran part of the way with Foxworth for a second run and that effort raised an additional $56,000. Oden's teammates from his first year at UMD, Tom Stone and Dave Baker, contributed money toward the scholarship and helped raise funds from others. Foxworth honored Oden for his "tireless humanitarian acts" and his "devotion to his community."

Harry Oden Scholarship funds grow every year, and nearly every year, except for 2020 due to the pandemic, Oden returns to Duluth to present the students with their awards.

Making A Change

In 2020, still happily retired in Milwaukee with his wife, Willa, Oden tells about the students he encouraged to go to college.

UMD wasn't the only recipient of Oden's dedication. "I've helped over 1,000 students of color, as well as white students, get into college, not just at UMD but into colleges and universities around the country," he says.

"I'm not going to get rich from it," he continues. "I get rich because I've touched so many lives, not just as students, but adults too. I've been blessed in a lot of ways."

Oden's commitment to helping students is a testament to the vow he made to his late father. Oden pledged he would always treat people the way he wanted to be treated, and he would always be willing to give something back. Remembering his father's words, Oden says, "After my last basketball year, I promised that I would never let a person of color go through what I went through at the university."

Oden also quotes Mark Twain, "The two most important days in your life are the day that you were born and the day that you found out why." Oden says, "People ask me when did I find out that important day in my life." Oden remembers two moments. "I think I found out what I was supposed to be doing on the first day I had a basketball in my hands in high school, and again on the day I got off the bus to attend the University of Minnesota Duluth. It was a combination of both."

by Myka Dixon

———

The banner photo at the beginning of the chapter is of Harry Oden in 1962.

20.

Lorenzo and Henrietta Music

Two bright stars get their start at UMD.

It's showtime. These were the words that Jerry "Lorenzo" Music and Myrna "Henrietta" Johnson Music heard constantly; the words that they fell in love with; and the words they would continue to hear for the rest of their careers. The couple's story starts at UMD, where they were stars, both on and off the stage.

Act I: The Set-Up

Myrna and Jerry grew up performing. They were both active in theater throughout their early years and high school. Jerry "Lorenzo" was born as Gerald David Music in Brooklyn, New York in 1937.

When Jerry was eight years old, his family moved to Duluth,

Minnesota, where he attended Central High School. While there, Jerry was a part of nine theatrical productions and was voted "wittiest student" by the class of 1955. He also worked at KDAL-TV holding cue cards for announcers. After graduation, he came to UMD as an undergraduate student, majoring in English and speech.

Henrietta Johnson Music, born Myrna Johnson in 1939, was also raised in Duluth. Her first theater performance was as the Hunter in the second grade in a production of *Snow White and the Seven Dwarfs*. She also attended Denfeld High School, however, it was not until 1958, when Myrna graduated from high school and came to UMD, that the paths of these two ambitious stars would collide.

Act II: Duluth Performances

While at UMD, Jerry and Myrna dove headfirst into their passion for theater. It was during rehearsals for the "smash-hit" musical comedy *Guys and Dolls* that the two first became an item.

A 1959 *Statesman* review of the performance says, "As the Hotbox chorus girl who had been engaged for 14 years, Myrna Johnson gave a brilliant performance as the female comic lead. She achieved a wonderful Bronx atmosphere in her voice, character, and movement. Jerry Music, as Nathan Detroit, broke the audience up with laughter with his perfect sense of comedy which more than made up for his lack of voice. Perfect coordination was found in his sense of timing."

The dynamic duo captivated and entertained Duluth audiences by performing in both informal and staged productions, and Jerry took the limelight again in the role of Anthony in the fall 1959 production of *Antony and Cleopatra*.

Jerry thrived in the spotlight. He spent the majority of his time playing banjo and performing comedy. One could catch him in the act at the Duluth Owl's Club and Eagle's Club, as well as at UMD in the cafeteria, or for groups, such as the faculty wives' tea. If people would watch, he would perform.

In 1959 Jerry left Duluth. In spring 1959, Jerry traveled the coffeehouse circuit in Los Angeles, Phoenix, Lake Tahoe, and Vancouver British Columbia. Myrna stayed at UMD, but she stayed busy. She performed as part of a trio, called the Coquettes, in the Homecoming Variety Show in October.

When Jerry returned to Duluth for his wedding to Myrna, he couldn't resist collaborating with fellow UMD performers. On the Thursday before the wedding, he and folk singers Hal Segal, William "Rusty" Gilchrist, and bongo player Stuart Johnson invited students to an afternoon "hootenanny" on campus. That evening Jerry presented a free "Evening with Music" performance in Kirby Ballroom. He and Myrna were married the following Saturday, November 5. Soon after, she joined him in his travels.

Next, Jerry performed in San Francisco's "Purple Onion," the college club that featured the Kingston Trio and Mort Sahl. That's when Jerry's act changed from "beatnik" to black tie.

The couple spent years traveling the country, giving performances at various nightclubs in the United States. Their act had the unique combination of folk music and comedy and they became known for their wit and Jerry's banjo. The move to fame did not stop the Musics from returning to their Duluth roots. They came back in October of 1961 to perform for UMD's homecoming dance.

After a 1964 tour of Japan with the USO, they returned to Duluth a 12-day engagement at the Duluth for Flame nightclub.

Act III: Hollywood

The couple eventually changed their names to Lorenzo and Henrietta Music and produced their talk, music, and comedy show in 1976, The Lorenzo and Henrietta Music Show. The show only lasted for about six weeks, but it acted as a launching pad for Jerry's television career.

Lorenzo joined the writing team for *The Smothers Brother Comedy Hour* and *The Mary Tyler Moore Show*, and created and wrote for *The Bob Newhart Show*. He also gave his vocals to the character of Carlton the Doorman on the television show Rhonda, a spinoff of *The Mary Tyler Moore Show*.

His career garnered accolades. In 1969, Lorenzo won an Emmy award for comedy writing on the *Smothers Brothers Comedy Hour* and in 1982 he landed the memorable role as the voice of Garfield on the TV series *Here Comes Garfield*. He won a second Emmy Award in 1984 for co-writing the Garfield special, *Garfield on the Town*. He ended up voicing the part of Garfield for over 115 episodes.

The Closing Act

Henrietta and Lorenzo eventually settled down in Los Angeles, California, where they had four children. They lived in California for the remainder of Lorenzo's life, but they never forgot their Duluth story. The couple would often return for family visits and class reunions, and they would light up the room with one of their acts.

One of Lorenzo's last visits to Duluth was in 1998. He returned for a final time to visit with UMD faculty and staff in the Kirby Rafters. Lorenzo passed away at the age of 64 on August 4, 2001. He is survived by Henriette, his children, and his unforgettable career.

by Izabel Johnson

_____

The banner photo is from the publicity photo for a return engagement at UMD.

21.

Bringing Civil Rights to Duluth and UMD

William Maupins, champions civil rights.

The year was 1965. Boxes were stacked high around Bill Maupins. Hundreds of items, including furniture, clothing, food, and school supplies, filled the loading area.

Volunteers worked alongside Maupins, arranging the items in the back of a semi-trailer. The shipment was on its way to deliver goods from Duluth to civil rights workers in Mississippi.

Maupins was the Duluth NAACP president from 1958 to 1969 and he worked at UMD from 1951 to 1982. This 1965 mission, to send support to the people in Mississippi who were fighting for voting rights, involved both his NAACP and his UMD roles.

Maupins encouraged UMD faculty, staff, and students to make

donations. He also rallied the NAACP community, the congregation at Duluth's Temple Israel, and other organizations to join in. They filled the entire truck.

The trip was more complex and more dangerous than a simple delivery. In the early 1960s, hundreds of people who dared to fight for civil rights for African Americans had been killed by the KKK. Violence in Mississippi was reported on the news every day.

In spite of the danger, UMD Chaplain Brooks Anderson, a friend of Maupins, was compelled to help the civil rights movement in Mississippi. Anderson and several UMD students, including Deanna Johnson, Orlis Fossum, Darlene Keeler, and Kenner Christensen, elected to follow the truck to Jackson, Mississippi. There, they heard about the now-historic march from Selma to Montgomery.

That took them another 200 miles, where they joined Martin Luther King, Jr. and many national leaders on the march.

Born in Duluth

Maupins' story starts in a hotel in Duluth, where Maupins was abandoned as a baby in 1922. He was taken in by a young woman, who died a short time later. Maupins was then adopted from an orphanage by a married couple. His adopted father was an elevator operator and shoe shiner at the Duluth Hotel.

Maupins went on to attend Central High School. After graduation, he served in the United States Navy during WWII and later went to UMD. Just three years later, in 1951, Maupins was a college graduate with a degree in political science.

Service to UMD

After graduating from UMD, Maupins began work as a janitor on campus. This didn't last long though, because Maupins' drive and intelligence were recognized. He soon landed the position of chemistry laboratory supervisor.

In the 1950s, the faculty and staff were so impressed by Maupins that Provost Ray Darland added affirmative action duties to Maupins' role. Duluth activist Claudie Washington says, "Bill noticed young people with promise and made recommendations to the UMD administration. I personally know over 40 people who were hired at UMD because Bill Maupins spoke for them."

The Life of an Activist

During his early years as a UMD student and later on employee, Maupins saw injustices taking place against African Americans and others. He felt he had a duty to speak out and take action.

"Many avenues are closed to Negroes," Maupins said in a Statesman article in 1947. "For one who seeks to prove his status on the basis of his college preparation, the opportunities are limited."

In 1958, Maupins ran for a position with the Duluth NAACP on the platform of fair education, housing, and employment for African Americans. He won, and in 1963, he became the NAACP president. This provided Maupins with a platform to do groundbreaking work as a civil rights leader.

Fighting Discrimination

Maupins and the NAACP were active in voter registration. They launched several initiatives, including one that helped to register nearly 100 African American voters in 1964.

He worked with the State NAACP to make recommendations for a state fair housing ordinance and to fight for the eventual national Fair Housing Act of 1968. In Duluth African American renters and buyers faced widespread discrimination in housing.

The NAACP files are full of deplorable incidents. One occurred when a young African American man was cheated out of his apartment rental and deposit after the landlord found out the man was an African American. Without a housing ordinance, renters had no recourse.

Another was the hateful vandalism of an African American family's home in the Lakeside neighborhood of Duluth. Racial slurs were spray-painted on all sides of the house. Even the sidewalk was covered.

Inspiration for Many

In his later years, people often visited Maupins in his home. Portia Johnson, a member of the ISD 709 Desegregation/Integration Council, and a City of Duluth civil servant commissioner, would stop by often. "Bill would sit in his favorite rocking chair and listen to our struggles on affirmative action. He was always good at working out strategies."

Maupins passed away in 1992, but he left a legacy of positive change. His influence is still felt by people in the city of Duluth and at UMD.

by Izabel Johnson and Cheryl Reitan

———

The banner photo is of William Maupins in a UMD chemistry laboratory.

22.

The Library Responds to the 1960s

Creating a space for diversity and inclusiveness.

In 1967 and 1968, UMD students were conscious of a shift in American politics. The editorial pages and news pages of The Statesman covered the civil rights movement and the struggle for social justice.

Many UMD events and activities included topics about diversity and injustice. In April 1967, James Meredith, the first African American to attend the University of Mississippi, spoke at UMD on "Racial Peace in America." After Martin Luther King, Jr. was assassinated in April 1968, UMD students raised money for the Martin Luther King Memorial Fund. That month, they also brought Dick Gregory, a comedian and civil rights speaker, to campus.

The George Bonga Room

Changes at UMD became more permanent when, in April 1969, UMD opened a Black cultural center for students, staff, and faculty at UMD. Called the George Bonga Room, in honor of a Negro-Indian voyageur in Minnesota during the 1800s, it was located in the UMD Library, which is now named Kirby Plaza. The library housed the George Bonga Collection, which contained books, magazines, and newspapers on African and African American topics; and it featured a framed portrait of Dr. King.

The Duluth community got involved. Mrs. Marjorie J. Wilkins, president of the Duluth Chapter of the National Association for the Advancement of Colored People (NAACP), presented UMD with a check for $100 to buy additional materials for the center.

UMD Librarian Rudolph Johnson said, "We are indebted to the NAACP and many students and citizens who have made it possible for us to make these purchases which greatly enhance our... library."

A Significant Place

Carrie (Maupins) Lindahl '69 and her sister, Sylvia (Maupins) Herndon '71, recognized the importance of creating a gathering place for Black students.

Their father, William Maupins, was a respected UMD staff member and president of the Duluth NAACP from 1958–1969. He also approved.

Lindahl remembered the George Bonga Room and regrets only having a few short months before graduation to use it. "We were pleased the administration and the library recognized the importance of a welcoming place for students."

Herndon says, "It was an enjoyable space. It was so comfortable;

Black students gathered for discussions, and speakers met with students there, over coffee and cookies, after events."

Outloud at UMD

Two notable speakers arrived at UMD soon after the George Bonga Room opened. They were Julian Bond and Rufus Mayfield.

A civil rights leader, Bond was a member of the Georgia House of Representatives and co-founder of the Student Nonviolent Coordinating Committee or SNCC. He spoke on politics and race in September 1969.

Mayfield appeared on the Kirby Ballroom stage in November 1969. He caught the nation's attention when he worked for justice in the case of a tragic shooting in Washington, D.C. A police officer shot Mayfield's friend in the back after an altercation over a 29-cent package of cookies. The friend died.

Mayfield continued his work for justice. He joined another civil rights champion, Marion Barry, to establish Destiny-Pride, a school and work program for 1,400 Black youth in Washington D.C.

Alumnae Remember

Herndon worked as a student worker in the scholarship and loans office and graduated with a degree in speech in 1971. She came back to UMD as an employee and one of her tasks in 1976 was to author a document for UMD entitled, "Recruiting and Retaining Black Students at UMD: A Handbook." It outlined strategies for creating a welcoming campus and called for the hiring of a full-time Black recruitment officer.

Lindahl graduated from UMD in spring 1969. She went on to receive her law degree in 1972 from the University of Minnesota and practiced law in Hawaii and Minnesota. Herndon went on for a master's degree from the University of Washington, Seattle. She worked in higher education and social services administration.

Diana (Coleman) Kelly married UMD football great Glen Kelly '71. She earned an undergraduate degree from the University of Michigan-Flint and a master's degree from Eastern Michigan University. She says that she and her husband are "happily" retired.

by Cheryl Reitan

––––––––––

The banner photo is of Diana (Coleman) Kelly as she reviews one of the books in the George Bonga Collection.

23.

1st Street Gang's Legacy

Groundbreaking student organization celebrates 50th year.

On Monday, May 4, 1970, the 1st Street Gang had an intramural softball game scheduled for 5 pm. As students finished their classes, members gathered on "The Ledge." That was the granite window ledge that looked out on Lake Superior, a perfect place to sit and watch students pass through the Kirby Student Center.

1st Streeters, wearing their signature white jerseys, which were traditional game-day attire, arrived as they finished their classes. Among them were two cousins, Tom Larson '73 and Bob Hofstrom '74, 1st Street Gang founding members. "We all made it a point to wear our jerseys to games," said Hofstrom. "We came out to cheer for our teams, the men's and the women's." The

Kirby Rafters lounge area was popular, complete with a fireplace, burgers from the short order kitchen, and beer.

Challenging the Frats

Hofstrom says, "The Gang started as a rap against the frats." In those days, UMD intramural sports were dominated by fraternities. "Before the 1st Street Gang came along, if you wanted to play intramural sports you had to join a fraternity," Hofstrom said. "We formed our 1st Street teams to challenge this situation." The "frats" had several teams. The May 3, 1970 Statesman lists intramural teams with names including Gamma, Phi Chi, Alpha Nu, Sigma, and Beta.

The Gang recruited student-athletes and soon took the lead in the standings for intramural ice hockey, floor hockey, basketball, golf, bowling, softball, and broomball. Both the women and men played in several sports.

A Changing World

The 1st Streeters stuck together. A group of men and women lived together in a house up the hill from the Pickwick, 502 East 1st Street. Later, they moved to 1818 E. Third Street and 322 N. 21st Ave. East.

Larson recalls, "We became mavericks, and in an awkward way we became the 'anti-frat' movement. Maybe it was the Vietnam War and the era of protesting that made it seem the right thing to do. We broke the lock on who ran campus life by starting our own group and using our own ways of operating."

The U.S. was changing, and the 1st Street Gang was helping UMD catch up. The fraternities and sororities didn't appeal to everyone and often came off as too exclusive.

"Bob and I worked together to foster and build an organization that we were proud of," Larson said, "It has a lasting legacy. It was my first taste of discrimination based on gender, and when I look back at how women were held back in many endeavors such as athletics and business–it was strictly gender-based. The Gang's inclusion of women changed my view of the world order forever."

Kristen "Fanny" (Thorberg) Swan '75 agreed, "As a woman coming of age, I was never more respected, cared for, and encouraged than by this band of brothers."

Creating Community

The 1st Street Gang embraced women as equal partners in their organization, as participants, players, and officers. Men and women supported each other, rooted for each other, fished, camped, hiked, and skied together.

They hosted "epic" themed parties at the 1st Street Gang houses, and planned elaborate parties together. The Greaser Party ('50's style), the End-of-the-World Party (dress as something or someone famous), Snark Parties (face painting), and the Pajama Party (pajamas only) stand out. An annual Smelt Fry Bash and the annual 1st Street Banquet were legendary. Long Duluth winters brought cribbage tournaments, euchre tournaments, and rounds of the 500 card game.

Later Years

The 1st Street Gang continued off and on for over 35 years. Children of some original members of the group have attended UMD and revived the Gang, although it never achieved the size and status it had when it started.

As 1st Streeters left UMD, families and careers took over. Yet, they still kept in touch. Many landed in the Twin Cities and got together for golf, hunting and fishing trips, poker night, and barbecues. They celebrated with organized events and informal gatherings.

Scholarship and LSBE Support

The year 2020 marks the 50th Anniversary of the 1st Street Gang. In all of those years, the Gang has never stopped supporting UMD.

In 2002, Geoff Spencer Memorial Scholarship in the Labovitz School of Business and Economics (LSBE) was established to honor 1st Streeter Geoff Spencer's memory. From the initial contributions of $36,000 and through additional contributions from members and investment earnings, the fund has grown to over 130,000. Since its inception, they have awarded UMD students nearly $45,000 to business students and in recent years, $5,000 to education students. It is one of the largest scholarships awarded in the LSBE at UMD, at $5,000/year. The education scholarship was created five years ago and continues to award an education student $1,000 each year. In 2009 LSBE dedicated the "First Street Gang" seminar room in their new LSBE building.

A Legacy

"I made 20 of the best friends a guy could have," Larson said. "I will always have their back as they have mine." To Larson, he found more value in what he learned from the Gang than what he learned in class. "It was the socialization, planning, and following through, that became the main posts of my life and career. These were the men and women who I have cherished my entire life and made me who I am today." That sentiment is still echoed today by many of the men and women members of the 1st Street Gang.

by Cheryl Reitan

———

The banner photo is of the First Street Gang intramural hockey team: Front to back — Tom Moynihan, Tom Larson, Dave Settergren, Bob Hofstrom, and (net) Bob Nelson.

24.

Filming a 1972 Thriller at Glensheen

You'll Like My Mother **flick brought Glensheen to life.**

"You'll like my mother," is what Francesca, played by Duke, was told by her late husband. Pregnant with his child and inspired by his words, she goes to Minnesota to visit her mother-in-law, played by Rosemary Murphy. Francesca is greeted with such a cold welcome, she wants to walk back to the bus station in a blizzard. Her mother-in-law is insistent that she stays the night and by morning Francesca has many questions, as well as a suspicion she may never be able to leave.

Released in the fall of 1972 and directed by Lamont Johnson, *You'll Like My Mother* is a fantastic look at Glensheen and its historic furnishings, yet in a different context. Many will find it refreshing to see the home filled with daily life again, even if it is just as a backdrop for a thriller movie.

Duke, who has returned to Duluth several times, said she enjoyed working on the production. "Duluth is terrific," Duke said at the time of the filming, "I'm not crazy about the cold, though."

Filming at the Glensheen Mansion

The Congdon family was approached by Universal Studios-Bing Crosby Productions to film on the site. The family was promised $7,500, which is worth about $46,000 in 2020. Surprisingly, Elisabeth Congdon, daughter of the late Chester Congdon, and her staff, still lived on the estate during the filming. "I don't know how they convinced her," stated Lori Melton, who was the marketing director of Glensheen in 2012. "As far as I know, she was a pretty private person."

Melton was responsible for putting together a 40th-anniversary event revolving around the movie. In 2012, Glensheen hosted a special *You'll Like My Mother* tour of the mansion with Easter eggs from the movie scattered throughout the mansion. The event ended with a showing of the movie.

Christa Lawler, who wrote about the event for *Duluth News Tribune*, stated that the baby in the movie was played by a Duluth native, Laura Adams, who was less than a month old. Laura's mother, Viola Adams, attended the special Glensheen event. She reminisced about how much of the filming revolved around her daughter. "Shooting hinged on baby Laura's naps to make sure they caught her hungriest cry."

The Film's Reception

The film received mixed and often positive reviews. "The story that follows is full of holes and not too full of surprises, and it is all developed in a screenplay that might most charitably be described as awkward... But there is also a visual density that is genuinely cinematic and that makes location shooting (in a real turn-of-the-century mansion in Minnesota) seem worthwhile," wrote Roger Greenspun of the *New York Times* back in 1972.

Where it "fails as a movie," as Greenspun claims, "it makes up for as a piece of history." Jim Hefferman, who was a reporter for *Duluth News Tribune* back when the film first debuted, said "the star performer has to be the Congdon home and carriage house." He continues, "For so many Duluthians who have admired it from the outside, it will be a treat to follow the color camera through its paneled corridors, carved stairways, and beautifully appointed rooms."

About Glensheen

Glensheen is the Historic Congdon Estate of Chester and Clara Congdon, at 3300 London Road. It was given to UMD in 1968, although Elisabeth, the youngest daughter of Chester and Clara Congdon, was allowed to live there through a life estate. Five years after the movie was filmed, in 1977, tragedy struck. The house became the site of the infamous murders of Elisabeth and her nurse, Velma Pietila, who were killed by an intruder.

In 1979, the mansion opened to the public. UMD operates it as a historic house museum and in recent years, over 100,000 visitors have toured the house and grounds. Even before the donation of the home to UMD, the congdons supported the university in other ways. "The family was very active in private giving with the University," said Dan Hartman, Glensheen's former director.

by Ellie Mercil

———

The banner publicity photo shows actors Dennis Rucker and Patty Duke (right) and an unidentified man (left) at a break between filming.

25.

Milestones and Celebrations

Alumni are the living history of UMD.

In 2020, in the midst of the COVID-19 pandemic, UMD celebrated 125 years of history. The year honored the academics endeavors, the dynamic alumni, and all of the achievements that continue to transform and benefit society.

UMD's story began on April 2, 1895, when Minnesota Governor David. M. Clough signed legislation approving the creation of the State Normal School at Duluth. In 1921, the Normal School became the Duluth State Teacher's College and in 1947, the teacher's college was named the Duluth Branch of the University of Minnesota. Over that time, there have been many anniversaries worth revisiting. Two notable events include UMD's 1995 celebration of its 100th anniversary and UMD's 1972 commemoration of 25 years as a University of Minnesota campus.

100 years of celebrating people, ideas, and achievements

The centennial celebration began years before the anniversary. Neil Storch, history professor, and Ken Moran, UMD photographer, embarked on a massive project, to write the 100-year history of UMD. Entitled, UMD Comes of Age: The First One Hundred Years, the book was published in 1995 and served as one of the focal points for many of the anniversary gatherings.

As the anniversary year loomed, a group of over 30 people came together to plan the events. Alumnus Harry Oden, the celebration chair, along with Diane Fay Skomars, alumna and director of UMD University Relations and Development, worked with alumni, staff, and friends to plan UMD's 100th-anniversary celebration in 1995.

Lucy Kragness, also an alumna, who worked at UMD as the alumni director and later as the chief of staff, was a member of the team since its inception. She reminded everyone that, "Alumni are the living history of UMD." She wrote those words in 1995 in another alumni publication, Celebrating 100 Years: UMD Duluth.

That publication has a history as well. Alumnus Steve Fox, the publisher of Minnesota Monthly magazine, helped UMD arrange for the piece to be inserted in an issue of Minnesota Monthly, which was distributed across the state.

Kragness, who wrote the prominent alumni section of the piece, visited the Minnesota Monthly office. "Steve was a lot of fun to work with," she says. She also enjoyed working with the magazine staff to help put the publication together.

And there was cake! The group planned reunions, dinners, homecoming, and other festivities. The main event was held on March 31, in the Marshall Performing Arts Center. Hundreds came to celebrate. Speeches and entertainment joined Michael Pagan's jazz ensemble, Synergy, and two slide presentations on the history of UMD.

25 years with full university status

UMD marked its milestones with pride. A 25th-year anniversary observance (1947-1972) honored the formation of the University of Minnesota Duluth. Celebratory dinners, campus events, and several cakes marked the milestone. There were gatherings at Eastcliff in St. Paul, hosted by Malcolm Moos, president of the University of Minnesota, and a recognition by the Board of Regents.

On June 30, 1972, faculty and staff members with 25 years of service were special guests of Provost Darland at a 25th-anniversary event.

Celebrating UMD's Impact

All of these celebrations are fitting reminders of the importance of UMD. As time passes on, the UMD community continues to celebrate Duluth residents, who supported its growth, the academic environment that fostered inquiry, and the alumni who have made a lasting impact around the world. Go Dogs!

by Cheryl Reitan

———

The banner photo was taken at the 25th Anniversary of the name change to UMD. It depicts Chancellor Ray Darland (far left) and University of Minnesota Regent Richard Griggs as they serve anniversary cake to Regent Frederick A. Cina (far right) and his wife, Ruth.

26.

Anishinabe Days

Alumni tell the story of the early years of the American Indian Studies program.

May 1973, David "Niib" Aubid (AA '92, BA '12) was a little late to the Kirby Ballroom for the Anishinabe Days Pow Wow. It was a Friday evening, and the room was full.

Niib, who was a UMD student at the time, is from the Mille Lacs Band of Ojibwe. He's from East Lake, a community that spoke Ojibwe and practiced their cultural traditions. That night, he was bringing the pow wow drum and a van full of drummers for the ceremony. Jay Yaag, an elder, and John Martin, an Ojibwe singer who taught traditional songs, were in the group.

On the way to the pow wow, their van had a flat tire. When they took out the spare, it was flat too. They had to roll the tire to the nearest gas station in Cromwell to get it fixed. When they finally arrived, Niib and his group were relieved to see that the festivities hadn't begun and people were still arriving.

Paul Buffalo, an American Indian elder and spiritual leader from Leech Lake, was performing a ceremony, sanctifying the area. Niib said, "Paul had on a headdress and was shaking a rattle near the floor, blessing the space for the dancers."

Many were in native dress, a few in full regalia. There were many Shawl Dancers and one of the male dancers was wearing a bustle, a large shield of eagle and hawk feathers, worn at the back.

That pow wow was one of the first Annual Anishinabe Days Pow Wow. Vern Zacher (AA 67 BA'72) explained, "One week every spring, we held Anishinabe Days." There were films and speakers each day. In 1975, they brought in Pulitzer Prize winner M. Scott Momaday to talk about his book, The House Made of Dawn.

"It was a strong time for American Indian students at UMD," Vern said. "It became a focus for students in Minnesota and North Dakota." UMD has hosted pow wow's for more than 20 years.

The Early Days

Jeff Savage, along with Niib and Vern, recently shared the story of American Indian Studies at UMD. Jeff is director of the Fond du Lac Cultural Center and Museum, and he attended UMD in the 1970s. The men give a lot of credit to George Himango.

George Himango returned from a tour in Vietnam in 1970 and with the encouragement of Ruth Myers, a woman known as the grandmother of American Indian Education in Minnesota, enrolled at UMD.

The year George arrived, only two American Indians had graduated from UMD. George recruited 12 friends to come to

UMD, and they put together a student organization, the Anishinabe Club.

Classes and Outreach

Beginning Chippewa was taught by Art Gahbow and Ralph Fairbanks. Those classes were on the fourth floor in Humanities, along with most of the American Indian Studies classes. "We took over a lab. We listened to recordings of people talking in Ojibwe," said Niib. "The teacher could coach each student, one at a time, through headphones."

In April 1972, American Indian Studies (AIS) was founded, and by October 1972, it became a program within the Division of Social Sciences. Its first director was Robert Powless, a member of the Oneida Tribe.

Niib gave high marks to one class, American Indians in the 20th Century. "It was taught by Dr. Powless," he said. "We learned a lot ... about Hiawatha, the peace chief of the Iroquois tribes, and the Great Law of Peace, the oral constitution of the Iroquois Confederacy." Other classes included Legal Aspects of Indian Affairs, Early Indian-White Relations: An Indian View, Teaching the American Indian Pupil, and Indian-White Relations 1776-1887.

The History and Culture of the Ojibwe class brought in the community. Visitors included Paul Buffalo, Roger Fairbanks, Tim Roufs, Don Murdock, Ruth Myers, Billy Blackwell, and Betty Gurno. In addition, students were visited by a dance group with Mary Howes, Roger Shaibaish, and John Martin.

The AIS students were extremely active. George, Vern, Clyde Atwood, and Ray Murdock met with the medical school and social work staff to provide them with a greater understanding of cultural differences. George and other students in the program, Ed Howes, Nora Gallaher, and Roberta DuFault, tutored American Indian inmates in Sandstone Prison. Vern remembers, "We went up to Enger Tower one year to protest Columbus Day." The Wounded Knee occupation in South Dakota in 1972 was in world news and also had the attention of UMD students.

There are a lot of people to thank for the success of the 48-year old AIS program. The first AIS Annual Report is dedicated to George F. Himango and Geography Professor Fred T. Witzig. Vern remembered, "Julia Newels Marshall and women at the Duluth Women's Club supported American Indian students." Many more people contributed to its successes through the years, including Rick Smith and the American Indian Learning Resource Center and the directors of the Center for American Indian Health.

The 48-year old AIS program is still strong. The program joins over a dozen American Indian programs on the UMD campus and hundreds of alumni from those programs remember the classes and American Indian traditions at UMD.

by Cheryl Reitan

——

The banner photo is Niib, a UMD student at the time. Information from this story came from the Archives and Special Collections, Kathryn A. Martin Library, University of Minnesota Duluth.

27.

Elizabethan Dinners

Fyne Arts: A 16th-Century Feast at UMD

Minnesota's first Renaissance Festival opened in Chaska, Minnesota in September 1971. Dozens of Renaissance events around the country joined Minnesota by offering dinners, jousting tournaments, royalty parades, art fairs, and festivities.

Early on, UMD jumped off the castle tower into the Renaissance world with an annual Elizabethan dinner led by Vernon Opheim, a UMD music professor and the director of choral music.

Jerry Kaldor, who graduated from UMD with B.A. in music in 1976, was one of the performers at the 1975 Elizabethan Dinner. He also joined the cast in the '70s and '80s when he came back to graduate school. Later, he enjoyed a long career as a music teacher in the Hermantown schools and a stint as choir director at the College of St. Scholastica. Kaldor was honored in 2018 as he became a member of the UMD Fine Arts Society of the Prometheans.

From 1974 to 1987, UMD's Elizabethan Dinner entertained with food, wandering minstrels, a court, and jesters. Kaldor became one of the Madrigal Singers, who performed the vocal chamber music called madrigals, and told a narrative story, similar to dinner theater. He had fun. "The Elizabethan dinners profoundly affected me," he says, "As I learned it, I became immersed in it and I fell in love with the music."

Kaldor enjoyed the performances and mingling with the crowd. Many were dressed in 16th-century regalia. "Each night as we got dressed in costume," he says. "As singers and actors, we took over the room. It was a great feeling to interact with people having so much fun."

When it came time for "Ye Order Of Feast," some guests, who wanted to be authentic, tackled their prime rib with a spoon or even their fingers. (Forks were only beginning to be developed during the late 16th century).

The Kirby Ballroom was brought back to the 1500s. That gave community members and students, faculty, and staff, the opportunity to live the way royalty did during the Elizabethan period.

In 1975, Tom Barber, who played the lute, and Lauri Wilson joined Kaldor. The evening included a six-course meal for $7.50. Guests started with a cordial cup of wassail and gave a toast of greeting and health. The main course included a salad, Yorkshire pudding, a vegetable, and prime rib of beef. Dessert was a flaming fruit pudding and the breads included an old English recipe for a whole hearth bread.

Professor Opheim, the director of choral music, took the helm each year, melding dialogue, acting, and song to unfold the stories.

"Dr. Opheim was a big person with a big presence," said Kaldor. "Without him, there wouldn't have been an Elizabethan Dinner. He brought his passion for the music and the pageantry alive in his students. Through all the years of the dinners, he was the constant. With an intense devotion to artistic excellence, he inspired countless students to share the music and the magic with countless attendees."

With the drive Professor Opheim brought to the effort, the event grew in popularity. He took on Cris Levanduski, a member of the University Singers, first as a student volunteer and later as a community volunteer, to help with the production and to develop the scripts. The University Singers, a group of 50-plus members all participated. Everyone got involved, from serving the food, creating the set design, making the costumes, handling the lights, and other tasks.

As the years went by, costumes and entertainment became more elaborate and the meal price went up. The Elizabethan Dinner was held in the spring, and for Duluthians, as well as royalty from the distant past, it was a cause for celebration. "Courts celebrated in great style with a big feast, good company, lots of laughter, and music," Opheim remarked in a 1975 Statesman article.

The UMD students thrived as the Duluth community embraced the unique event. "No one had ever experienced anything like it before," Kaldor says. "Every night was more enjoyable than the next."

by Jack Harrington and Cheryl Reitan

——

The banner photo shows the actors playing "royalty" at one of the Elizabethan Dinners.

28.

The Outdoors Comes to the Campus

Bagley Nature Area: Free fun!

It was late winter of 1972. Susan (Elliott) Lyons '77 was a junior in high school visiting her brother Scott Elliot '76 at UMD. They spent a day at Rock Hill doing what Sue loved, skiing! Somewhere along the way, Sue doesn't know when, a photographer snapped a photo of her (see the banner photo, above).

"Bagley meant free fun," Sue says. She loved Rock Hill in the winter.

Sledding held its own appeal. Sue has a few confessions to make about her time at UMD, and she is glad that, "The statute of limitations has expired on taking cafeteria trays from the dining hall." Sue and her friends used them as sleds. "They were a creamy yellow color, and they worked great."

While she Sue was attending UMD, Rock Pond had been enlarged to its current size of 1.3 acres. It was also a popular destination for Sue. One year she took a canoeing class from Eleanor "Ellie" Rynda, the legendary administrator in collegiate athletics and an assistant professor in the health, physical education, and recreation department.

"We had to take the class before we could go on a UMD canoe trip to the Boundary Waters," Sue says. She remembers hearing Professor Rynda standing on the shore. "She called out the canoe strokes, 'J stroke, C stroke, forward feather stroke,' barking like a drill sergeant." It was worth it to get the reward: canoeing and camping in Northern Minnesota with friends.

Sue has to mention the statute of limitations again. "Once we portaged an eight-gallon keg of beer into the Boundary Waters."

After receiving the 1975 Bulldog Award and graduating Magna Cumme Laude from UMD in 1976, Sue went on to marry her classmate Scott Lyons.

Bagley Nature Area History

The history of the Bagley Nature Area begins when the University of Minnesota Duluth was established in 1947. Part of the negotiations to transform the Duluth State Teachers College into UMD was an effort by Richard Griggs to give UMD the land for the new university. Griggs corralled a group of Dulutians to purchase the 176 acres of land where UMD stands today. That act sealed the deal for the Minnesota legislature to create UMD.

The Griggs gift inspired the Bagley family to make a gift of their own. In 1953, Dr. and Mrs. William R. Bagley and Dr. Elizabeth C. Bagley presented UMD with 17 acres of land as a gift. The property adjoins UMD, across St. Marie Street from the campus buildings.

The Bagley family stipulated the land, first called Rock Hill and

University Park, was to be used "to add to the welfare of the student body and also enjoy its resources" and it mentioned creating acreage as "a nature center." William Bagley was respected in Duluth and was well-known for his interest in wildlife conservation.

The property needed improvements. In 1961 Paul Munson, a biology professor, called on UMD to get rid of the "dumps and wilderness camps" and remove trees that "obstruct the view of Duluth harbor." Over the years proposals for several uses were made, but UMD refused, opting instead for retaining its natural environment and using the land for recreation.

Recreation included a ski hill where, at first, a basic tow rope was built. In 1968, UMD received grant funding and built trails, bridges, and dug a pond to its full 1.3-acre size. They also built a ski tow power house.

Downhill skiing ended in 1975, but cross country ski trails, hiking trails, canoeing, and camping thrived. That year, on March 12, 1975, the name was changed again. It went from Rock Hill and University Park to the WR Bagley Nature Area.

In 2010, an environmental classroom opened near St. Marie Street.

In recent years, Bagley has served another purpose. The college students in the American Indian Science and Engineering Society (AISES) at UMD have been holding a sugar bush in the Bagley Nature Area. They teach other UMD students, and children in the community, about the Native American way of tapping maple trees to make maple syrup. One student in the club, Ron Willis, (shown above) led the sugar bush project at Bagley in 2019.

Honoring Our Past

The land that is now the Bagley Nature Area, was once "covered in white pine," says Wayne Dupuis '87, the environmental program manager for the Fond du Lac Band of Lake Superior Chippewa.

He shared insights about the Duluth that existed hundreds of years ago. "Many of the trees in the white pine forest were over 400 years old." They grew to heights of 150 feet. Bagley pond flowed into the headwaters of Tischer Creek, "where trout climbed uphill from Lake Superior," he says.

Deer and small animals, like rabbits and fox, are still plentiful in Bagley. Even bear and moose occasionally make an appearance. But centuries years ago, porcupines, mink, marten, fisher, partridge, and many more animals were plentiful.

Bagley Nature Area and UMD reside on what has always been indigenous lands. In 2019, UMD adopted a formal Land Acknowledgement stating that the campus occupies traditional, ancestral, and contemporary lands of indigenous people. The university has gratitude and appreciation and honors the Indigenous people who have been living and working on the land from time immemorial.

by Cheryl Reitan

——

The banner photo shows Susan Lyons who hadn't enrolled in UMD at the time. She was visiting her brother for a weekend trip at UMD.

29.

Support for Diverse Students

Linda Belote launches diversity and inclusion efforts.

The Marshall Performing Arts Center was packed with students chattering excitedly as they waited for the curtains to open and the music to begin. It was Sept. 23, 1992, and it was time for the Andean band, Inti Raymi, to play for the students. The band's name means Festival of the Sun, and their music, which consisted of pan pipes, drums, and stringed instruments, brought plenty of sunny moments to campus. The musicians, from Ecuador, Peru, and Bolivia, filled the theater with Andean folk music. The next day they performed again in Bohannon 90.

Linda Belote was hired in 1988 as the director of the UMD Achievement Center and assistant vice-chancellor of academic administration. Belote was a Peace Corps volunteer in Saraguro, Ecuador, along with her husband, Jim Belote, in the early 1960s.

Some thirty years later, in Duluth's Canal Park, Belote heard something that suddenly reminded her of South America. She heard the sounds of pan flutes and saw the Inti Raymi band. As she talked to the band members, a friendship was formed, and the band agreed to perform at UMD. Year after year, they returned. Along with other events, Inti Raymi's performance brought a spirit of Multiculturalism to the campus.

Belote's role in the Achievement Center was to lead and supervise several units: the Supportive Services Program, which provided academic support and study skills; Career Services; the Access Center, which provided services for students with disabilities; and African-American Student Services. She quickly realized there were major components of UMD's multicultural population that needed to be better served.

From 1988 to 1996, Belote wore multiple hats. When she arrived she said, "I was shocked how few resources were allocated for students of color compared to universities in the rest of the state." She went right to work making changes.

In early 1989, Belote created positions for two work-study students to provide some services to two underserved groups because there were no funds for regular salaried personnel. The students hired were Susana Pelayo-Woodward for the Hispanic-Latinx students and Thao Ho for the Southeast Asian students. Together they contacted the students who had self-identified as members of those populations and called separate meetings of these two groups. Pelayo-Woodward and Ho each soon had a cadre of active students from across the campus. Belote said, "These young people not only wanted their services, but they wanted the campus to know they existed. They worked to create celebratory cultural events to educate the campus community about their cultures."

Staff Changes

In the spring of 1992, the Achievement Center received financial support from the Twin Cities Diversity Office to hire one full-time salaried professional for each of these groups. Pelayo-Woodward had left UMD and earned a master's degree by this time. She responded positively when urged to apply for that position. She was hired. A separate search yielded Koua Vang for the Southeast Asian students. Looking back on those days, Belote said, "Both were excellent choices."

In the fall of 1992, UMD restructured its senior administration and the position of director of the Achievement Center was newly located under the vice-chancellor for academic support and student life. Belote was promoted to associate vice-chancellor and given enough funding from two UMD sources, Academic Administration and Academic Support and Student Life, to be able to continue with the two new resource centers, plus a new tutoring center.

Belote's energy to advance diversity never faltered. During her time in the Achievement Center, she worked with African-American Student Services staff members Henry Banks and Ken Foxworth, as well as Vang and Pelayo-Woodward. Along the way, Foxworth was replaced by Saadia Wiggins in 1996, and Wiggins was replaced by Festus Addo-Yobo in 1997.

In 1991, Linda Belote with the UMD African-American students who performed a Reader's Theatre. The event was instructed, coached and directed by Dr. Annjennette "Anjie" McFarlin, a faculty member at Grossmont College. Another guest, Theresa Ford, assisted with the instruction and also performed. Ron Sundstrom, BSA president at the time, impressed Belote with "his powerful voice for oratory."

Belote championed more than diversity programs. She served on the UMD Commission on Women, a campus group seeking to improve the climate for women. Pay equity was the real issue. All faculty and staff women had received equalizing pay adjustments upward in 1989-90 due to a successful lawsuit initiated by women at the UM-Twin Cities. In a Statesmen article, published on January 28, 1993, she said, "We can't rely on dead, white males for our scholars and culture; there is a great deal of diversity in America. Equality is something one has to keep vigilant about."

When Belote left the Achievement Center in 1996 to return to the full-time teaching of her first love, anthropology, the Achievement Center was restructured.

Big changes continued. The multicultural team was formed, consisting of Addo-Yobo, Vang, and Pelayo-Woodward. It continued for many years, with Pelayo-Woodward in the capacity of lead staff. Pelayo-Woodward said, "UMD received support from Dr. Rusty Barcelo, the University of Minnesota associate vice president for multicultural and academic affairs, to secure funding to staff the UMD multicultural programs." In 2000, Angie Nichols arrived as the Gay, Lesbian, Bisexual, and Transgender Services director, and in 2004 the Multicultural Center was created on the second floor of Kirby Student Center.

UMD's effort received a new name, Office of Cultural Diversity in 2009, and Pelayo-Woodward was finally named the director, after taking a leadership role in UMD's multicultural efforts for 20 years.

As the years passed, the Achievement Center worked closely with American Indian programs at UMD, on the academic side as well as the student support side.

Programs to Change the Campus

Over the years, UMD's diverse community formed many organizations on campus. These included, Hispanic/Latino/Chicana, Latinx, African-American, Africana, Black Students,

Southeast Asian, Southeast Asian-American, and others. What didn't change was the advocacy for recruitment and retention of students of color at UMD and the frequency and popularity of their events. Fiestas, Soul Food dinners, Kwansas, Chinese New Years, and Vietnamese New Years were joined by the annual International Taste of UMD and many more celebrations.

In 1991, Ban Van Tran, president of the Southeast Asian Organization, helped organize the first Vietnamese New Year event. He discussed the importance of the cultural dragon dance in the Statesman. It is supposed to "scare the bad spirits away so luck will come back at the beginning of the new year," he said. Other entertainment included a magic show, a karate demonstration, and a fashion show showing traditional as well as contemporary dress.

Some of the celebrations earned epic status. The theme of the Soul Food dinner in 2000 was "Unity." Over 300 people attended the dinner but the organizers were hoping for more attendance from other campus groups and sororities/fraternities. Along with the Southern cooking, there was poetry and dance. Nicoshia Boulton, BSA President at the time, noted that "without unity and love the soul of mankind is nothing."

The Many Lives of UMD Fiestas

Belote remembered the first Fiesta in 1989, an event which was organized by several students including Pelayo-Woodard, who was a student at the time. The entertainment for the three-hour event included two ethnic dance troupes and three bands. One of the bands was The Latin Fire Trio, who had worked with artists such as Jennifer Lopez, Mark Anthony, and Gloria Estefan.

Another early Fiesta was especially memorable. One student's father was a chef from Mexico working at a Twin Cities restaurant that specialized in Mexican cuisine. He traveled up to Duluth to create authentic food for the Fiesta. In later years, the UMD catering staff created authentic food themselves, using student advice.

In 2006, the 17th annual Fiesta was held with the theme "Fiesta de las Americas." Belote said at that time, she had attended 15 of the 17 events. The 2006 get-together focused on celebrations from Bolivia, Peru, Mexico, and Brazil.

Doing the Right Thing

As it grew, UMD's multicultural services and programs brought in thought-provoking keynote speakers and challenging informative events. Their supportive academic services helped recruit and retain students from a huge variety of backgrounds and supported them on their journey through undergraduate and graduate programs.

by Cheryl Reitan, Ellie Mercil, and Bailey Jacobson

———

The banner photo shows performers at a 1990 Fiesta in the Kirby Ballroom.

30.

Radio for Wise Women

Student voices find air time in KUMD's studio.

Susanna Frenkel, a UMD alumna and a member of KUMD's "Wise Women Radio" team, was the publicity director for a big event, a Holly Near concert on November 10, 1982.

Airwaves, the KUMD monthly newsletter, called it "the musical event of the season," and hailed Near as a "champion of women's rights, gay rights, anti-war protests." Near was on a 50-concert international tour that had already taken her to an audience of 200,000 people in West Germany.

The evening of the KUMD concert, Frenkel was confident of the concert's success. They pre-sold enough seats to break even. After the sound check at the Thorpe-Langley Auditorium on the

University of Wisconsin-Superior campus, Near needed a place to get ready.

Frenkel's apartment was in Superior and as the evening unfolded, "My husband remembers Holly ironing her blouse in our kitchen," says Frenkel. Before Near donned her concert outfit, "We fed her something to eat," Frenkel recalled. Pre-event jitters ended and the production staff of KUMD's "Wise Women Radio" joined the Twin Ports community to enjoy the concert.

Community was central to the formation of KUMD. Frenkel graduated in 1975 with a history major. Her time at UMD was spent following her passions. She did pregnancy counseling for the UMD Women's Resource Center and was one of the writers for a Statesman column, "The 51% Minority." Judith Niemi, an English professor, encouraged Frenkel to take on serious topics for the column. Editor Judy Cavanaugh inspired Frenkel when she renamed the paper The Statesperson for several 1973 fall editions.

After graduating from UMD, Frenkel worked in Duluth. She was a Vista volunteer at the North Country Women's Center, and worked at the CHUM homeless shelter and a rape crisis center, before and after heading off to Goddard College. There, she received a masters degree in women's studies in 1978.

Back in Duluth, she says, "my first memory of KUMD was walking into the little closet space off the VenDen." She met Tom Livingston and Phil Glende there.

The prospect of starting a radio show for women began percolating after Cathe Hice-Hall wowed the audience with an all-women music program for the 1980 Fall Marathon. By early 1981, "Wise Women Radio" debuted with a Sunday afternoon women's affairs program, which was repeated on Tuesday afternoons. After the public affairs program, women announcers followed with women's music.

"KUMD was so low tech," Frenkel says. "At first, we could only queue up records. Then there was reel to reel. We cut the tape of an interview and pasted it together."

But there were memorable moments both on and off the air. "I played a Whoopi Goldberg record, and there was some wording that was unacceptable to the FCC," Frenkel says. "I got in real trouble then." Once, the "Wise Woman" crew sold anatomically correct gingerbread cookies in the Kirby Student Center as a fundraiser. "We made a lot of money and got a lot of attention for that," Frenkel continues.

After the birth of Frenkel's first child, "Wise Women" played less of a part in her life, but the show continued with staff and strength into the 1990s.

KUMD TIMELINE

KUMD began in 1957 as the Broadcasting Club at UMD. Its first staff included Bruce Elving, Doug Hedin, Dick Gottschald, and faculty advisor Robert Haakinson. The signal from the lower campus was weak. One account tells of "a mischievous UMD student," who ran a wire from the station antenna to the window and dropped it. All of a sudden, the signal could be heard all over Duluth and Superior. That is until the FCC picked up the signal.

In April of 1958, the FCC assigned the call letters "KUMD."

1960s

Studios moved from the Lower Campus to the basement of the Education Building on the new campus. But the station didn't operate at all in 1963 and struggled to stay on-air in 1964. Walt Kramer worked his way up from announcer to become the student general manager in 1968.

1970s

In 1971, Mike Dean was the station manager, and by the

mid-1970s, Phil Glende, David Tuenge, and Tom Livingston had joined the station. UMD Provost Robert Heller paid $95,000 to purchase WDTH from Minnesota Public Radio in 1974. At first KUMD staff broadcast the same programming on both stations.

Producer Jean Johnson with Shawn Keenan Gilson, who covered news and public affairs. Gilson investigated Northland stories and repeatedly broke news in the national press.

Livingston became station manager in 1976 and In the fall of 1979, a "marathon" fundraiser brought in more than $15,000 in pledges.

1980s

In 1980, WDTH added staff, received new funding, and qualified for support from the Corporation for Public Broadcasting. Engineer Kirk Kersten brought new expertise to the often jerry-rigged broadcast and studio equipment, and Jean Johnson started as a producer.

Community support during pledge drives rose steadily. The station moved to the Humanities building, and a remodeling project produced a larger control room, better record storage, and improved studios.

New programming included "Wise Women Radio," a public affairs and music program by and for women. The station also began broadcasting NPR programs including "All Things Considered," "Morning Edition," and "Fresh Air." Other national programs included "Blues Stage," "Echoes," and "Mountain Stage."

In March of 1982, a new license renamed the station KUMD. In 1984 Paul Schmitz became station manager. Later Donna Neveau joined the staff as a wonder woman with many titles. Bob DeArmond and Helen Prekker joined the outreach staff. News and public affairs coverage increased with Kathleen Anderson, Shaun Keenan Gilson, and Janice Windborne. A weekly call-in program, "Talkline," brought UMD topics to the community. Volunteer

Laura Erickson began producing "For the Birds," which continues to run.

1990s

In 1991, Lisa Johnson was hired, and she created "Northland Morning," a mix of locally hosted music, features, and local public affairs. It took the place of "Morning Edition."

Laura Erickson's "For the Birds" aired on KUMD in 1986 and now is the longest running radio show about birds in the U.S.

In the same year, KUMD joined five other national stations to pilot "The World Cafe," a mix of jazz, acoustic, and world music. Volunteer John Bushey brought the long-running "Highway 61 Revisited," a celebration of all things Dylan. The late-night "RPM" show highlighted Minnesota bands and "U-Talk Radio" showcased issues debated by UMD students. In 1992, with encouragement from the UMD University Lesbian, Gay, Bisexual Alliance, volunteers produced "This Way Out Northland." A year later, students from the Black Student Association offered "Two Hours of Power," featuring urban contemporary music.

2000s

Christine Dean returned to KUMD in 2000, after working there as a student in the late '80s. Program director John Ziegler expanded involvement with regional musicians by producing CDs called In Studio Sessions: Live from the KUMD Music Room.

KUMD consistently won recognition as the best station with the best programming in town and announcers gave increasing attention to local artists. In 2006, Mike Dean came on as general manager. The following year, the station celebrated its 50th anniversary with two concerts. Vicki Jacoba came on as station manager in 2008. New staff: Maija Jenson, Ira "Mimmu" Salmela, and Chris Harwood, joined Christine Dean, and turned the focus more toward students and academics.

In 2009, Scott "Starfire" Lunt, creator of the Homegrown Music Festival and a member of the band Father Hennepin, produced "The Local," with music and interviews with regional musicians. That year, KUMD was producing new local programs, such as "Radio Gallery," "Women's Words," "Women's History Month," "Ojibwe Stories," and others. Erin Welch oversaw a new website, while Emma Deaner served as the membership and marketing assistant.

2010s

KUMD entered a new decade by offering 24-hour programming. Student programming grew as Sam Ginsberg brought a program, "The Basement," along with creativity and drive. He organized a scavenger hunt in which the clues were broadcast on-air. In March of 2013, the Basement went national on MTV-U's "College Radio Countdown." It was the only university to broadcast from an ice house!

2020

There are now more than 100 students and community volunteers involved with the station. KUMD broadcasts 95,000 watts of power and reaches a 60-plus-mile radius surrounding Duluth, and it can be heard online from anywhere in the world.

by Cheryl Reitan

———

The banner photo shows Susanna Frenkel, Kathleen Ryan, Kath Anderson, and Jean Johnson in the KUMD studio.

31.

Boosting Minnesota's Economy

UMD alumnus Rolf Weberg tells NRRI's story.

The late 1970s and early 1980s were a troubling time economically for Duluth and northern Minnesota as a whole. The decline in natural resource-based industries, and especially the taconite mining industry, brought the economic life of the Northland to a dire situation.

With no industry to fill the void, scores of Iron Rangers and Duluthians chose to move away in search of better opportunities. As they did, many saw a billboard at the top of the hill that read, "Will the last one leaving Duluth please turn out the lights?" Visionaries at the state legislature and other community leaders saw many avenues to economic development.

They knew the natural resource portfolio of northern Minnesota did not begin and end with taconite.

Weberg at UMD

It was during this uncertain time when Rolf Weberg came to the University of Minnesota Duluth. He arrived in 1978 from Mankato with the intention of going into medicine. The son of two chemists, he had no interest in following their footsteps.

"You don't know how determined I was to not be a chemist," Weberg jokes. In addition to the requisite science and math classes, he also took trumpet lessons from Dr. George Hitt and loved playing the trumpet in the jazz ensembles and numerous bands and orchestras. He seriously considered becoming a music major.

His tune changed upon meeting chemistry professor Robert Carlson, Ph.D. "He's the guy that turned me around in a matter of 24 hours and got me excited to be in the lab," says Weberg. Carlson has a reputation for inspiring students in the 50 years he taught at UMD.

Known for always learning each student's name, Carlson had a knack for leading his students into discoveries and captivating them with the enthusiasm of what is possible. "Bob is a scientist who could have gone to any university in the country," Weberg says. "Instead, he committed himself to UMD and Duluth, and I was lucky enough to run into him."

Weberg would meet regularly in Carlson's "time capsule of an office" and the two would discuss chemistry, ideas, and ongoing projects. "It was always an invitation, not an order," Weberg says. "He always encouraged exploration, questioning, and sharing of knowledge."

NRRI Beginnings

At the same time, Weberg was learning in the Carlson chemistry labs, civic, business, government, higher education, and labor leaders were exploring incentives to help the economy through applied research. In 1982, during Weberg's senior year, Rudy Perpich was running for governor. Perpich proposed that a center be established to do research on such resources as peat, biomass, forest products, water, and minerals.

Back at UMD, with Carlson's encouragement, Weberg graduated with a degree in chemistry in 1982. The next year, the Minnesota State Legislature established the Natural Resources Research Institute (NRRI) at the University of Minnesota Duluth.

Weberg went on to earn a Ph.D. in inorganic chemistry from the University of Colorado Boulder in 1986. He followed that with two post-doctoral appointments, ending in 1988.

Life with Dupont

Weberg spent the next 25 years in the R&D division of the DuPont Company, a global leader in scientific research and innovative products. While in the role of Global Technology Manager for the Building Innovations Business Unit, he was approached about becoming the executive director of NRRI. Weberg dismissed the opportunity at first — he was really enjoying his position with DuPont.

"At DuPont, I had wonderful research opportunities," Weberg remarks. "I got to experiment with neutron beams at the Oak Ridge National Laboratory. I worked to create new materials and processes to make them. I traveled the world and worked with amazing people. I had ended up with the job I wanted — I wasn't looking to go somewhere else."

NRRI's Early Years

When Mike Lalich took the helm of NRRI in 1984, the focus was for scientists to turn basic concepts into practical ideas to create jobs using Minnesota's natural resources like iron ore, peat, and timber.

NRRI worked to improve products made from Minnesota wood fiber and continued research on making better and more cost-effective taconite to feed the domestic steel industry.

Researchers at NRRI were also instrumental in Great Lakes ecosystem rehabilitation efforts. They continued work on developing new products made out of peat and restoring peat bogs.

From massive projects like mapping, and defining copper, nickel, and other valuable metals deposits to diverse projects, such as developing a process to recycle mattress springs or creating fast-growing poplar hybrid stocks.

The NRRI Draw

Weberg had turned down the job three times before being persuaded to come to Duluth and look at what NRRI had. "As soon as I got there, I flipped again," Weberg says. "Minnesota, the state that invested in me and my education, was still suffering from some of the same problems as when I left. I saw challenges here that I was prepared to help with and that would give me an opportunity to give back."

Weberg credits many reasons for his eventual decision to take the job, but chief among them was the people. "These people were so damn dedicated to a cause, it was hard to say that I didn't want to be a part of it."

Through the late fall months of 2013, Weberg struggled. He questioned leaving his successful career and the many people all over the world who he cared about. He finally decided on Christmas Eve that he would take the position in Minnesota. "I came up from Minneapolis, in March through a snowstorm, to officially accept the job, and thought what the hell did I just do?"

And then, "I remember driving over the hill and seeing the port, and I knew it was going to be okay."

NRRI Today

It has been nearly seven years since Rolf Weberg took the helm of NRRI. He has added his strengths to the shape of the organization. NRRI has a staff of some 130 people with an annual budget of about $15 million and five integrated research platforms: Applied Ecology & Resource Management, Minerals & Metallurgy, Materials & Bioeconomy, Data Collection & Delivery, and Commercialization Services.

NRRI has two semi-industrial sites; one in Hermantown and one in Coleraine. The Hermantown site holds many of the research laboratories while the Coleraine site houses their Minerals and Biomass Conversion Laboratories, with industrially relevant scaled equipment for bench-to-pilot research. NRRI also operates a Fens Research Facility in Zim, Minnesota to study peatland restoration.

"NRRI is committed to build on Mike's legacy and drive the transition towards a nationally recognized research institute," Weberg says. "We were created by the legislature to help make good decisions regarding forestry, forest products, soil, land, minerals, and water." Under his watch, NRRI has invested heavily in supporting infrastructure to help the researchers. "They need to do what they do best — research."

Weberg has helped guide NRRI to a position as a premier source of integrated research solutions, "The ability to leverage a multidisciplinary staff to translate an idea into a demonstration and develop it — partnering broadly to go from bench to demonstration scale — differentiates us from many other resource research institutes in the nation," he says.

Improving the Economy

The vision that drives NRRI research is to discover the economy of the future, and that requires a lot of work. "We need to be looking forward and engage everybody in that discussion." Weberg continued. "NRRI is meant to understand the challenges, frame the issues, and provide unbiased research to help guide and grow the economy."

In a constantly evolving world, NRRI is helping Minnesota stay competitive. and Weberg says he is proud to be a part of it. "I made the right choice, and I haven't looked back. Life has been a circle — coming back to Duluth to join NRRI and re-engage with Bob Carlson is a rare opportunity, and I'm lucky to have it."

by Jack Harrington

———

The banner photo is a historic photograph showing the ore docks, the St. Louis River, and Lake Superior.

32.

Powering the Economy

David McMillan's start in business and economic research

David McMillan stood on giant piers of steel that stretched out into the St. Louis River and looked over Duluth and Lake Superior. He was on top of the Canadian National Railway (CN) ore docks. A few feet from him were the train tracks, and hundreds of feet down below him was the berth where the 1,000-foot ore carriers received their loads.

When the CN offered McMillan and the Saint Lawrence Seaway Development Corporation (SLSDC) a tour of the docks, he jumped at the opportunity. "I've driven under the railroad tracks that lead to the docks hundreds, maybe thousands, of times and always wanted to get up there," he says. From that high vantage point, it seemed that the history of the region played out before him ... the mines, the railroads, the docks, the ships.... forestry, wood pulp, and wood product plants... and all the jobs and people that held it all together.

BBER and UMD

McMillan, a UMD 1983 alumnus and member of the University of Minnesota Board of Regents, came to UMD from the Twin City suburbs in 1979 to study economics and history. In his senior year, he joined the Bureau of Business and Economic Research (BBER) as a student researcher. The job fit with his interest in economics. He worked with Professors Jerrold Peterson and Richard Lichty, and other members of the Economics department faculty, on an input/output model, measuring regional economic activity, among other projects.

He found the work fascinating. "It gave me a really good grounding in the area's resource and service-driven regional economy," says McMillan. They did studies on the indirect and direct output of manufacturing and paper mills. And the models led to actual projects. "The Louisiana Pacific plant outside of Two Harbors, that produces wood trim and siding, came out of that research," McMillan says. He found delight in the formulas. "X amount of capital investment is likely to create X amount of jobs; I just love that stuff," he says.

Petersen and Lichty encouraged McMillan to look at a Ph.D. and a career in academia, but there was a stronger field calling, the practice of law. McMillan applied for several law schools and got into a few.

He anticipated the final word about his start date from his number one choice, the University of Minnesota, where he was on the wait-list. That's when things got interesting.

Peterson and Lichty were so impressed with McMillan's work as a researcher, they offered him a one-year term faculty appointment as a research fellow. The law school wait-list uncertainty made McMillan take the job offer seriously. There was one more factor to consider, McMillan had started spending time with Cari Charboneau, his future wife, and she was going to be in Duluth until her graduation the following year. "All the priorities changed," says McMillan. He accepted the BBER offer.

Back in Duluth

After law school in Minneapolis, McMillan joined the legal team at Minnesota Power and then began his adventures as an executive of Minnesota Power. In 2011, he was elected to the University of Minnesota Board of Regents. Over the course of his career, he has served the community. McMillan currently serves as chair of the SLSDC Advisory Board and previously served as the board chair of the Minnesota Chamber of Commerce, UMD's Natural Resources Research Institute, the Area Partnership for Economic Expansion, and Goodwill Industrial Vocational Enterprises. He is also a past member of the Duluth Entertainment Convention Center's Board of Directors and the Board of Directors of St. Luke's Hospital.

"If the BBER funding had not occurred back in 1983, I don't know what direction my life would have taken," McMillan says. "It certainly wouldn't have revolved around resource-based industries and the economic impact they have on northeastern Minnesota."

He calls it a "full circle." He and Cari agree, "We're blessed to call Duluth home."

BBER TIMELINE

Early 1960s

Cecil H. Meyers, UMD professor of economics at the University of Minnesota Duluth, and Glen O. Gronseth, a research analyst for the Duluth office of the Minnesota Employment Security Division, began producing a powerful and popular research report – the Duluth Business Index (DBI).

The DBI, first published in 1964, provided an overview of the Duluth economy from the measurement and analysis of fifteen components that included coal, postal receipts, grain, and telephones.

These extensive monthly reports became sought-after tools for businesses and government and were later joined by the monthly publishing of the Duluth Retail Sales Index and the Duluth Hotel-Motel Tax Index.

1970s

Recognizing the need for a defined entity to oversee these extensive ongoing research projects, the BBER was officially established in 1970 through the appropriation of special monies in the amount of $10,000. Meyers was the first appointed director (1970–1979), and he also continued with full-time teaching responsibilities.

In October 1974, the Board of Regents approved UMD's academic reorganization and named the School of Business and Economics, with the BBER and the DBI fitting under that umbrella.

1980s and 1990s

Over time, the BBER gained the reputation as an unbiased and respected research entity and expanded its offerings to include cost-benefit analyses, input-output modeling, publications, forecasting, and more.

As requests for the BBER's research and analysis capabilities continued to grow, its structure was changed to employ a full-time director, full-time editor/writer, and a small number of undergraduate research assistants.

The business indexes that started it all continued to be pivotal data and information for the Duluth community and continued to be published until the late-1990s when it became increasingly difficult to gather the needed data.

BBER directors included Jerrold Peterson (1979–1983), Donald Steinness (1984–1990), Jerrold Peterson Interim (1990–1992) Kjell Knudsen (Acting 1993–1995), and Richard Lichty (1996–2003).

2000s

James Skurla served in the director role the longest, from 2003–2014. The current director (2014–present) is Monica R. Haynes.

Alumni and Accolades

Many of the BBER's former student researchers have gone on to have impressive careers, working at companies such as IBM, Boston Scientific, Google, and Cirrus Aircraft. One former student, Chris McIntosh, is now UMD's economics department head, and David McMillan is a University of Minnesota Regent.

Over the years, the BBER has taken on many large and notable research projects, some of which have had significant impacts on the region. Among them, a cost-benefit analysis of curbside recycling for WLSSD, a cost-benefit analysis of Reserve Mining, a study on the relocation of the I-35 Corridor, a cost evaluation of the BWCA, and a valuation of the Minnesota Public Library's Return on Investment. More recently the BBER has evaluated the impacts of the trade relationship with Canada, identified and mapped all employment service providers in the region, and evaluated the feasibility of mass timber manufacturing in the state.

Today

In 2020, the BBER provides economic information to the community in a new format, through its involvement in the Regional Economic Indicators Forum, a biannual event that highlights trends in employment, industry performance, business and consumer confidence, and local stock performance.

With her background in applied economics, Haynes has been increasing the BBER's scope of services. Some of these initiatives include conducting comprehensive surveys, utilizing additional modeling software, verifying economic impact studies from other entities, and forming partnerships with other University of Minnesota departments to offer additional services like GIS mapping and business retention & expansion.

Today's BBER isn't much different than its original iteration. It still seeks to provide research on economic factors affecting Duluth. But it has grown to provide research services for businesses, organizations, industries, government entities, and more for Duluth, the region, the state, and beyond.

by Cheryl Reitan with Jack Harrington

———

The banner photo shows the 1970 UMD Economics Department (l-r): Charles F,. Holt, Jerrold M. Peterson, Dennis L. Nelson, Cecil H. Meyers, David A. Vose, and Wayne A. Jesswein.

33.

Homework and Hockey

Mixing a degree in office administration with a zest for life

Sherri LeKang laughs when she tells the story of Bulldog Hockey and the 1984 Frozen Four. "The Bulldogs had beaten the Gophers, that was the gold standard," she says. The campus was buzzing because UMD was on its way to Lake Placid, New York, for the playoffs. Sherri was not about to be left behind.

She was in her junior year at UMD and forces had come together to create a certain vibe. Winters were long, and snowfalls set records. "We would stand in line for hours in Kirby to get student season tickets to the hockey games at Pioneer Hall." Weekend evenings started with finding a ride to the game and relaxing afterward at Grandma's Saloon or the Warehouse in Canal Park. Sherri also was friends with Tom Herzig, the hockey player from International Falls.

Sherri and Sue Brannon, her college roommate, didn't think twice about the trip to New York. They rode the student bus, a rented motorcoach. "We got on the bus early in the morning and arrived the next day." They drove through a blizzard in Upstate New York, but as one sports reporter said, it didn't matter because "the Duluth fans were delirious."

During the opening games, Duluth beat its rival North Dakota and Bowling Green trounced Michigan State. That left the Bulldogs facing the Bowling Green Falcons for the championship on March 24. Defenseman Tom Kurvers, who had just received the Hobey Baker Award, top scorer Bill Watson, and centers Matt Christensen and Tom Herzig all played a phenomenal game, with a tied score after the third period. That night, UMD played in the longest NCAA men's hockey championship game ever played. The Bulldogs went four overtimes before losing with a score of 5-4. "It was a pretty quiet ride home," Sherri says, "but it was a season we will never forget."

Hooters Broomball

Sherri started college life living in Griggs Hall and later at the Oakland Apartments. In her senior year, she lived in Capehart Housing on Arrowhead Road. She was captain of an intramural team called the Hooter Hunters and played broomball, floor hockey, and softball, competing against teams with names like the Outlaws and Amazon River Rats.

"A lot of my friends came from the Iron Range," she says. "Rudy Perpich was the governor and there was a lot of pride in being from Northeastern Minnesota." Sherri shared that pride. She had many relatives in Two Harbors. One weekend she traveled to Hibbing and learned how to make potica (a rich, thinly rolled sweet bread dough) with her friend Lisa Diehl and Lisa's mom. "We had to roll the dough out to stretch it," Sherri laughs. "We stretched the dough all over the kitchen."

A Life-Shaping Academic Program

In the fall of 1981, Sherri arrived at UMD, fresh from graduation from Fridley High School. At freshman orientation, she sat next to William Ellis, a classmate who became her lifelong friend, and told him about her plan. "I wanted to major in office administration and become a high school teacher who taught business courses." William and Sherri became good friends and William enrolled in the business and office administration program, too. "We've been friends ever since," Sherri says.

Sherri learned a lot from her professors, especially Tom Duff and Pat Merrier. Sherri appreciated Mildred Zoller, an instructor in the office administration. "She was a mother hen to us. 'Millie' invited us to her house in Lakeside for dinner, and she brought treats to work." Sherri says her teachers were the best people. "So much of what they taught me, I still use today."

The course was heavy in computer management and leadership. "We learned to look at the whole situation and decide what to do. By learning the tools for financial management and asset management, I blossomed."

The class was taught to assess the culture to come up with strategies to bring the project to fruition. "Above all, we were taught that people were the number one concern," Sherri says. "That lesson has taken me far."

"Right now, the world is facing the COVID-19 pandemic," she says. The lessons from her program at UMD are coming full circle for her. "The most important thing is how we take care of each other... How we stay engaged... How we come through these very tough times as a team."

During the summers, Sherri landed an internship with Medtronic, a global medical device company. "I developed a unique skill set in the Office Administration curriculum that was technical and included a great deal of focused communication training." Sherri was very organized, and she had "excellent grammar skills, which helped a lot."

After leaving UMD, her first job was at Health One, a not-for-profit group of hospitals, clinics, and other care centers from 1985 to 1991. She also earned a Master's degree from Metropolitan State University. Her next position was with Metropolitan Rehabilitation Services, a private forensic psychology practice, from 1991 to 2013. During that time, she was back at school again, this time for a master's in Higher Education Administration from the University of Minnesota.

Now Sherri is an administrative director with the University of Minnesota School of Medicine in the Department of Surgery. "I am so thankful I get to work with such incredible people," she says. She works closely with Dr. Sayeed Ikramuddin, head of the Department of Surgery, and former department head, Dr. David Rothenberger, who provides leadership as the senior advisor for Physician Well Being within the Medical School.

"I am blessed to work with our team of surgeon scientists, researchers, educators, and dedicated staff," she says. "Although we're isolated, we don't walk alone. It is empowering to empathize with others."

by Cheryl Reitan

_____

The banner photo shows UMD hockey players (from left) Tom Kurvers, Bill Watson, Matt Christensen, and Tom Herzig.

34.

Bulldog at the Helm

The conditions couldn't have been more favorable for the 12-hour job... until they weren't.

It was April, and scientists and crew members aboard UMD's research vessel, the *Blue Heron*, installing scientific equipment on the western arm of Lake Superior. "Everything went perfectly. The crew worked like a Swiss watch out there," remembers *Blue Heron* Captain Rual Lee.

But spring on Lake Superior can be volatile, and that volatility took hold as the *Blue Heron* turned towards Duluth for the 11-hour trip back to shore. "The wind switched, and it got worse. We ended up in a snowstorm – a gale with waves coming behind us," says Lee. Autopilot does most of the boat's steering, but the waves got so bad they started overpowering the system and Lee was forced to hand steer successfully back to shore.

Empowering Research

Growing up in Duluth, on sailboats and docks around Lake Superior, gave Lee the mental muscle needed to captain through the storm. And as a 1986 UMD grad, he has the added passion for the research that happens on his cruises.

Lee enrolled at UMD pre-*Blue Heron*, majoring in history and political science. The Large Lakes Observatory, where he would later work, wouldn't be formed for several years, but a formation of a different type took place. "Going to UMD becomes part of who you are. It affects the way you look at things and how you see the world."

After graduating, he worked with marine safety gear and in commercial diving. When the Large Lakes Observatory was looking for a captain for the predecessor to the *Blue Heron*, the *Noodin*, Lee was hired.

"The Best Part of the Job"

These days, excursions on the *Blue Heron* can last up to three weeks. In fact, a 2011 cruise brought them from Duluth, through Lake Heron, and into Lake Erie. This extended time gives Lee and his crew plenty of time to get to know the research and the researchers that are aboard. "That's one of the best parts of the job– to be able to hang around really smart people doing really interesting research."

Screens are set up in the *Blue Heron*'s galley kitchen where the crew and scientists talk about what they're finding over dinner. Lee's an optimal partner who makes sure that researchers are able to maximize their time on the Great Lakes, collaborating with chief scientists to find out what can be done in what order, depending on the weather.

And scientists can only use the equipment that they have with them, so the crew members are master improvisers... like the time researchers were coring, taking samples off the floor of Lake Superior with a giant straw-like tool, and the core catcher went missing, so they riveted together two pop cans.

"It's our mission – science support," Lee summarizes. It's a simple explanation for a role that Lee's taken to new depths in the name of impactful research.

Large Lakes Observatory Timeline

The move to create a UMD center to study Lake Superior began with a Lake Superior Water Policy Conference in 1988. With impetus from the conference attendees, chemistry professor and visionary Robert Carlson led the effort to establish an Institute for Lake Superior Research. In 1994, with financing secured, Professor Tom Johnson was recruited to lead the unit. The name was changed to Large Lakes Observatory and its mission was broadened to its current global scope.

The purchase of a research vessel in 1997 was the most significant early advancement. In her previous life, the *RV Blue Heron* was a commercial fishing trawler that fished the Grand Banks in the northwest Atlantic. Johnson and an LLO crew sailed it from Portland, Maine, through the St. Lawrence Seaway and across the Great Lakes to Duluth. During the winter of 1997/1998, the Blue Heron was outfitted for scientific research.

1998 brought the first scientific cruise on the RV Blue Heron as part of the Keweenaw Interdisciplinary Transport Experiment in Superior (KITES) project, a large NSF-funded project focused on better understanding water circulation in Lake Superior.

Under Johnson's watch, LLO grew in size and stature, and it maintained a strong focus on geophysical sciences because that was a unique and undercapitalized niche in large-lake science. LLO was instrumental in the International Decade for East African Lakes program during this time. Many internationally significant discoveries were made in that effort, including Tom Johnson's work on volcanic ash from the Toba supereruption in Lake Malawi.

In 2004, Professor Steve Colman was hired to lead LLO. The team of researchers launched much new work in Africa while establishing new observation platforms on Lake Superior. Faculty numbers grew and outreach programs were broadened.

LLO underwent a major renewal during the period of 2013 to 2016, replacing close to fifty percent of its faculty and increasing further in size. Residents and visitors to Lake Superior began attending a summer Science on Deck educational series. Beginning in 2013, LLO invited members of the public on board to tour the boat and learn about research and education on the Great Lakes. Professor Eric Brown served as interim director before Robert Sterner took over as director in 2014.

LLO has continued to grow and broaden. Active areas of investigation include paleoclimate, carbon cycling, geomicrobiology, water, and ice dynamics, benthos and plankton dynamics, and ecological stoichiometry. LLO is active in graduate curriculum reform in limnology.

Lake Superior has been a primary focus, but that hasn't stopped LLO scientists from conducting research throughout the world. LLO scientists have carried out major expeditions to the great lakes of the East African Rift Valley, Lake Issyk Kul in central Asia, Lake Nicaragua, Lake Qinghai in China, Great Slave Lake in the Canadian Arctic, as well as to smaller lakes around the globe.

by Lori C. Melton

——

The banner photo is the Blue Heron. Taken from the UMD University Marketing and Public Relations office.

35.

UMD's Early Title IX Timeline

Linda Larson, UMD, and changes in Women's Athletics.

In a world where gender discrimination in sports was common practice; in a world where women coaches were drastically underpaid compared to men; in a world where women athletes were far more rare than men; Linda Larson became the first coordinator of women's athletics at UMD.

Born to Play

Linda Larson was born in San Francisco, California, and raised in Chicago, Illinois alongside her twin brother, Don.

Growing up, Larson was always perplexed about why her brother got to join in team sports, but she had to sit in the stands. "I wasn't allowed to participate in sports but he could," Larson said.

Although a gifted student, Larson was always drawn to athletics. In high school, she was encouraged by teachers to pursue a more academic career path. She said that one of her mathematics instructors even wrote in her yearbook, "Why P.E.?" For Larson, the answer to this question was simple: "Because I wasn't allowed to do it. It was a challenge."

Larson studied physical education and administration and received a B.A. from Northeastern Illinois University in Chicago in 1971, and an M.A. from Ball State University in Muncie, Indiana, in 1972. She taught physical education classes as a graduate assistant while at Ball State. In September 1972, she was hired at Culver Military Academy in Culver, Indiana, in the new position, as girls athletic director and also coached volleyball, basketball, softball, and track and field.

A Career in Athletics

Larson came to Duluth and UMD in 1975. She said she "lucked into" the women's athletic coordinator position.

Larson remembers talking to Joann "Doc Jo" Johnson, a professor in the physical education academic program, who served in an ex-officio capacity on many athletic department committees. Johnson didn't tell Larson she had been hired at first. Larson remembers being introduced by Johnson to Ralph Romano, the athletic director and Bruce McLeod, the assistant athletic director, as they ate lunch is Romano's office. Johnson said, 'This is your new women's coordinator.'"

A Different Time

When Larson started at UMD, there were no paid coaches for women. Professor Bob Powless from the American Indian Studies program was coaching basketball for free and a graduate student was in charge of volleyball. The rest of the teams were coached by members of the UMD physical education faculty, Johnson (field hockey), Eleanor Rynda (women's and men's cross country, women's and men's indoor and outdoor track and field), and Mary Mullen (swimming and tennis.

Larson was hired as the women's athletic coordinator, but also saw the need for additional coaches. With no additional money available to hire coaches, Larson added coaching volleyball, basketball, and softball to her workload. Again, the existing model of women coaches volunteering to coach continued. Larson, like Johnson, Rynda, and Mullen, wanted to provide athletic opportunities for women at UMD, so they continued to volunteer their time and expertise to make it happen.

These four women sought to uphold Title lX which is a clause of the 1972 Federal Education Amendments. Title lX was signed into law in 1972. Its 37 words state that "no person in the United States shall, on the basis of sex, be excluded from participation in, be denied the benefits of, or be subjected to discrimination under any education program or activity receiving Federal financial assistance."

The women faced an uphill battle. Not only were there no paid coaches but women's athletics was hardly recognized. Larson said that when she arrived, UMD was in the process of moving Women's Athletics into the Athletic Department, which was Men's Athletics only. The larger gymnasium had "Men" written over the entry, while the smaller one had "Women." She met resistance to "having women involved in what was always the men's area," Larson said.

The funding for women's athletics was minuscule compared to the men's program. "Everything [in] the athletic budget… went to the men," Larson said. "Everything" meant all of the scholarships. That allocation was in direct violation of Title IX. Larson brought up some report discrepancies to Bruce McLeod, the athletic director at the time. She had received a copy of a document from the University of Minnesota Twin Cities that listed scholarship money that women at UMD received.

"Who's getting these scholarships?" she asked Bruce. "Women don't have any scholarship money."

McLeod's only response was, "Well, I guess we better be careful that we do our reports right." No efforts were made to rectify the situation.

Making Change

"I was just trying to find out information, a lot of times," Larson said.

"I think the concern was [that] I was rocking the boat." Larson faced massive opposition to full Title lX compliance. However, her strategy didn't involve overt struggles. Instead, she issued written reports and pointed out imbalances. At this time, there was strong opposition to Title lX from men's athletic programs at colleges and universities across the country. In 1988 the Civil Rights Restoration Act stated that Title lX applied to all programs and activities of any educational institution receiving Federal financial assistance. Failure of educational institutions to comply with Title lX legislation led to various lawsuits.

Larson's instincts were right, but it took 24 years after Title lX was adopted for the full story of inequities to be exposed. In 1996, some of the UMD women soccer players filed a Title lX lawsuit against UMD. It wasn't just women's athletics that suffered, it was the integrity of the program. As the March 1997 issue of Women in Higher Education reported, "At the University of Minnesota-Duluth, trouble in the athletic department kept growing." In August of 1996, "Bruce McLeod resigned amid charges of theft and diverting funds earmarked for gender equity to other accounts."

The challenges Larson faced did not keep her from doing her

job or speaking her mind. Throughout her career, she championed women athletes. She worked to expand women's athletic programming on campus, which was integral to the university's compliance with Title IX.

Making a Difference in Campus Life

During her 27 years at UMD (1975-2002), Larson served in many capacities. She coached softball (1977), volleyball (1976-81), and women's basketball (1976-80, 1981-84). In addition to her position as women's athletic administrator and senior woman administrator, she served on the NCAA Division II Women's Soccer Committee.

UMD has continued Larson's legacy. As of 2020, men's and women's scholarships are supported equally and nearly 170 female athletes participate in UMD's intercollegiate sports. Karen Stromme, who came to UMD in 1982 as Larson's assistant basketball coach, now serves as senior woman administrator as well as senior associate athletic director.

Larson did extensive work for women. On-campus, she worked diligently to improve the position of the Women's Resource and Action Center and served on the Commission on Women. Off-campus, she volunteered her time and served on the boards for the Northern Pine Girl Scout Council and the Duluth YWCA.

In 1999, Bob Corran, UMD's then new athletic director, nominated Larson for the President's Award for Outstanding Service to the University of Minnesota system. She was awarded this honor.

UMD also created a special annual award in Larson's name. It honors women at UMD who exemplify going above and beyond to benefit women at UMD. She was bestowed with the first Linda M. Larson Outstanding Woman of the Year Award in 2002. The recognition is still presented every year to women faculty, staff, and students. Larson often comes to campus to present the awards to the recipients herself.

UMD has given praise to Larson many times in the past and the 125th Anniversary of UMD offers one more opportunity to remember her contributions to equity in athletics.

by Izabel Johnson and Cheryl Reitan

––––––

The banner photo shows Linda Larson along with (l-r) Kelley Tralle, Julie Coughlin, and Amy Erickson as they celebrate advancing to the NAIA national tournament in 1993.

36.

Lost Architecture

UMD's Old Main joined lost historic Duluth places.

Tucked away on Twenty-third Avenue East and East Fifth Street in Duluth stand three red sandstone arches. They loom over the surrounding neighborhood with a story that some have forgotten. These arches belonged to the original UMD building, commonly called "Old Main." Before it belonged to the University system, it was Duluth's Normal School and later the Duluth State Teachers College. The building was designed by the architectural firm of Emmet Palmer, Lucien Hall, and William Hunt. Construction of the building started in 1898 and was abruptly halted by a fire in 1901 which gutted all progress. This wasn't going to stop Duluth from building their own Normal School, as they were desperately in need of one. The building was rebuilt and completed within the same year.

Finally, the Duluth Normal School opened in September of 1902. The school had ten faculty and just over a hundred students. As attendance grew, so did the need for more buildings and dormitories. The two neighboring dormitories, Washburn (1906) and Torrance Hall (1907), were designed by Clarence H. Johnston, who is best known for the architectural designs of the famous Glensheen Mansion.

In 1988, a UMD undergraduate research project titled An Historic Portrait of Old Main was written by Paul Edgbert Anderson, who graduated in 1989. There is some doubt that Anderson was able to enter the building, as UMD vacated it in 1985. Anderson examined the historical and architectural integrity of Old Main. He described the style used in designing this renowned building: in depth, a Beaux Arts interpretation of Renaissance Revival architecture. This style was "characterized by absolute symmetry, the uses of classical orders, and the concept of unity and the relation between the whole and its parts." Photos in the UMD Archives show simple decorative borders and Victorian-style light fixtures in nearly every room.

"Fortunately," Anderson wrote, "Duluth's 'Old Main' has withstood the times by escaping fire and demolition. The building gives the UMD campus historic identity and aesthetic integrity. With the acceptance of the complex into the National Register of Historic Places, it is obvious that the complex is historically significant."

Anderson spoke too soon. On February 23, 1993, the building burned to the ground.

After the Fire

The loss of Old Main was a shock to many UMD alumni. Ken Moran, a 1951 alumnus who served as the UMD campus photographer for decades, remembers the morning after the fire. "It was a little traumatic for me," he said. "That morning I heard on the news that there was a fire at Old Main. I thought I'd drive by with my camera and maybe I would see a blackened window someplace." Instead, Moran saw a smoldering ruin.

Later that year, Moran investigated some activity at the Laboratory School, which still stands next to the remaining Old Main arches. The Laboratory School's high chimney had been scorched by the Old Main fire and had to be taken down. Moran was expecting to see equipment erected on the site for pulling the tall chimney over. "I didn't see any equipment," he said. "Instead there were two men on scaffolding, taking the chimney apart, brick by brick."

"I'm glad they created a park on the Old Main grounds because people are still able to visit it," Moran said. "It's part of the memories of the people who went through school there."

Moran echos the words of countless alumni and community members, "It was a beautiful building."

by Ellie Mercil

⎯⎯

The banner photo is of the arches immediately after the 1993 fire that destroyed Old Main.

37.

Merrie Olde England

Students expand their horizons in the British Isles.

In 1980 the study abroad program to Birmingham, England began at UMD. Tourism to the U.K. began a steep incline that year, just as the first woman Prime Minister Margaret Thatcher took office. The Birmingham rock group, Duran Duran, was high in the world music charts… and going higher. The same year, Hercules, a bear, which had gone missing on a Scottish island during the filming of a Kleenex advertisement, was found!

In the U.S. and at UMD, Anglophiles were paying attention. When invited to sign up for the first UMD collaboration with the University of Birmingham, 50 students registered. This was the first program of its kind in the University of Minnesota system and it blasted off with a strong start.

Bob Evans was the program director for 1981-82, the second year of the program, and along with his wife, Mary, he served as the director two more times, in 1996-97, and 1999-2000. Thanks to Bob, Mary, and the other directors, students have memories of trips to London, historic sites, parties, and lots of group activities. At least 12,000 UMD students and 130 UMD faculty participated in the Birmingham study abroad program. It ran 31 years, 1980-81 to 2010-11, when it moved to the University of Worcester, for a time.

Bob and Mary Evans took students to Shakespeare's open-air Globe Theatre in London. After the guided tour the students got to go on stage.

Through the entire length of the University of Birmingham partnership, one UMD faculty member would go for the whole year as the director, and others came in for a term as teachers. With Bob's friendships, British faculty were recruited to expand class offerings for the students. The classes would typically relate to England and field trips with the faculty expanded the students' knowledge of the U.K.

Wordsworth and the Lake District

During the first weekend in Mary and Bob's 99-00 year in Birmingham, they took the students to the Lake District. The students stayed in a big camping lodge with lots of bedrooms and a big kitchen. "It was right on the lake, and it was beautiful," Mary says. The students made all of their own meals and invited Mary and Bob to join them.

The group crossed that lake to visit Rydal Mount, one of Wordsworth's two houses. They enjoyed a guided tour and even saw the bedroom where Wordsworth died. There were giant hills on Lake Rydal, and to the student's surprise, Mary and Bob kept up on the afternoon hike to the top of one of them.

Bob says, "The weekend was great because the kids got to know each other while boating, hiking, and cooking. It was the perfect opportunity to bond. We were so pleased that we planned the outing for the beginning of the year."

Birmingham's Fall Semester

Not long after classes started, Chancellor Kathryn Martin arrived. She traveled with College of Liberal Arts Dean Linda Krug and Vice Chancellor Vince Magnuson. Marilyn Russell-Bogle, from the library and American Indian Studies, Linda Belote from sociology and anthropology, and Bob who taught philosophy, already had the classes up and running. The visitors were treated to a party. "The students entertained us," Mary says. The camaraderie among the group was strong, due to the "lovely weekend" in the Lake District. "Some of them sang," Mary says. "There was piano playing and acting. Our visitors were really impressed."

The students wrote: "We would like to dedicate this year to two very special people in our lives… With Bob's philosophical life lessons and Mary's loving touch, they became exactly what we needed."

Bob and Mary invited the students to a party every month to honor the students who were having a birthday. Mary tried to make something that would remind the students of home, typically Mexican food, or spaghetti. The students were treated with gifts, cake, ice cream, and games. Bob and Mary designed this to help the students feel more connected to each other and have fun.

Birmingham Creates a Lively Backdrop

Mary and Bob enjoyed the city of Birmingham along with the semester faculty. Elizabeth "Betsy" Quintero, from education, and Judy Trolander, from women's studies, came in the spring. The atmosphere was marvelous," Mary says. "We ate Indian food a lot because it was really, really good and it was inexpensive." Fish and chips (French fries) were a favorite with the students. "We'd go into these little shops to order and then we'd find a place to sit outside or eat standing up." Mary and Bob took in the occasional concert at Symphony Hall, and afterward would often see students going out clubbing. The drinking age in England was 18, which was a big difference from Minnesota's drinking age of 21.

The Jacobean Aston Hall, in Birmingham, provided a great trip where students found bullet holes from England's 1643 Civil War.

A Visit to Wales to see a Resurveyed Mountain

The group traveled to Llansilin in Wales to see a land formation that was resurveyed for the designation of "mountain" rather than hill.

There was a novel and a film made about the adventure entitled, *The Englishman Who Went Up a Hill But Came Down a Mountain.* Everyone climbed the wrong hill but could see the mountain better that way.

Utensil Party Mash up

Before the students returned to the states in the spring, the students announced they were hosting a luncheon. Betsy, Judith, and Lynda, who worked in the program office, gathered at Mary and Bob's flat. First, students arrived with flowers and candy and escorted all off to House 10 where some of the girls lived. "There were four bottles of wine on the table, and different courses were served by the students," Mary says. There was a catch though. For each course, they were only allowed one utensil. So everyone was challenged to eat soup with a fork and salad with a knife. The students were all dressed up as waiters and waitresses. Bob says, "The whole event was a ball." After lunch, Bob and Mary were presented with a yearbook which was filled with dedications and pictures of the students.

The 1999-2000 Birmingham group saw an incredible array of

sites, made friends from around the world, and lived in the moment. Their dedication to reunions proves that memories and friendships can last a lifetime.

by Bailey Jacobson and Cheryl Reitan

————

The banner photo shows UMD students at the Jacobean Aston Hall, in Birmingham, UK. The students found bullet holes from England's 1643 Civil War at this site.

38.

A Jewel of Environmental Learning

Boulder Lake, citizen scientists, and bird nerds

Debbie Waters Petersen was the first UMD student director of the Boulder Lake Environmental Learning Center (BLELC). One of her most successful programs during her first year was a session on animal tracks. "Lots of people are interested in identifying animal tracks," she says.

And that February morning, about 60 people showed up for the program. "There were so many, we had to split them into two groups," she says.

Petersen arranged for an area trapper, Dan Crocke, to help with the session. A day before the class, he had placed bait across the bay from the Learning Center building.

The group found a lot to see. They found tracks of rabbits, squirrels, deer, fox, martin, and weasels. Most surprising were wolf tracks from a few wolves, coming directly at the bait in a straight line. "The tracks came from the other side of the lake, as far we could see," says Petersen. "They could smell the bait from that far. It was the coolest thing."

The joy Petersen found on the wild land was balanced out by the struggle of learning to be a director. "It was trial by fire; I was it," she says. "I was trained in biology and ecology, and I had to learn how to teach and master 1,000 other skill sets, too." She kept the books, found the instructors, led the sessions, and marketed the steady stream of public programs.

The moments of wonder made it worth it. Petersen tells one story after the next about those few years. There was the time instructor Judy Gibbs (UMD Environmental Education alumna) taught a program on wolves and ended by teaching the group to howl for wolves. "There were about 25 of us that night," Petersen says. "We drove in a caravan to the east entrance and got out and howled." Sure enough, the wolves answered back.

When Petersen was the director, the BLELC had the greatest density and diversity of songbirds in the State of Minnesota. She has lots of bird stories.

There was the time a group canoed across the lake to camp out, and they found a ruffed grouse and a nest of chicks. Once, she took her very young niece along on one of Boulder Lake's owl surveys. Surveyors used playback of owl calls to elicit a response from owls at designated survey spots. At one spot, they heard an answer. She and her niece witnessed two barred owls, a male and a female, calling to each other from across the road.

Banding birds loomed in her life. Petersen still conducts research on birds for UMD's Natural Resources Research Institute and other entities, but she got her start at Boulder Lake. She is now also a songbird bander, although owls are still special to her.

During owl irruption years, she and her friends would band Great Gray, Boreal, Snowy, and Northern Hawk owls. One time they banded "a ton of Great Grays," she says. A mouse served as the lure, and when the owl landed, they flipped a landing net over it and quickly attached a band to one of its legs before they released it.

Petersen was Boulder Lake's second director and first student director. She was also the first graduate student from the Center for Environmental Education, which is a part of the College of Education and Human Service Professions (CEHSP).

With a master's degree in environmental education from UMD under her belt, she spent 11 years at Duluth's Hawk Ridge Bird Observatory and now she teaches high school in Walker, Minnesota. "I teach all my ornithology classes how to band birds."

From the texts and emails she gets from former students, it's clear they enjoyed Petersen's classes. "I start every ornithology class by showing the motion picture, The Big Year. It's about three men who compete to see as many birds as possible in one year. And then, when Petersen's students are "pumped up," she teaches them how to identify birds by sight and sound, eventually moving on to banding songbirds and woodcock chicks. And, some of them become, as she says, "bird nerds."

About the BLELC

The Boulder Lake Management Area (BLMA) and its Environmental Learning Center is a "window" for various audiences to view full-scale, integrated natural resource management occurring in the BLMA using such things as interpretive trails, public programs, and formal environmental education activities.

The BLMA was conceived in 1988, was formally established in 1991, and contains over 18,000 acres of land and water, eighteen miles north of Duluth, Minnesota. The area is cooperatively managed for natural resources by the BLMA landowners: Minnesota Power, the St. Louis County Land Department, and the Minnesota Department of Natural Resources (MDNR). That set of partners formed an alliance with UMD's Natural Resource Research Institute (NRRI), and in 1994, Jerry Niemi, the director of NRRI's Center for Water and the Environment, brought Ken Gilbertson, the director of UMD's Center for Environmental Education, on board.

Over the years, workshops and speakers remained a mainstay, but several other larger programs have been offered, including the popular Master Naturalist Volunteer Training, Woodland Advisor classes, non-timber forest product workshops, and others. The number of participants has grown from a few hundred people a year to over 10,000. Many things have stayed the same, such as the Tracks and Traces outing, however, the number of workshops, hands-on training, and public events has grown.

Numerous scientific studies have taken place and are still underway, including the Great Lakes Worm Watch and a UMD Medical School Duluth and a Minnesota Department of Health project monitoring the status of mosquito and tick-borne diseases. In addition, external research partnerships have been added such as the Environmental Protection Agency Tree Swallow project to study potential impacts of polyfluoralkyl substances (PFAS), the Emory University's White-throated sparrow genetic study, and the University of Minnesota and Minnesota Department of Natural Resources' Jumping worm documentation.

There is still work to be done. The current director, Ryan Hueffmeier, says they are always looking for more organizations to conduct their research at Boulder Lake.

UMD Adds Education

Beginning in 1994, Gilbertson provided student directors to the BLELC. Except for the first director, Kent Montgomery, and NRRI researcher Cindy Hale, they were all graduate students in the Center for Environmental Education.

The list of student directors includes Kent Montgomery '94-'97, Debbie Petersen Waters '98-'00, Jeremy Solin '99, Dan Peterson '00, Sara Hanson '00, Mara Lundeen '01, Sara Lerohl, '02-'04, Megan Curtes '04-'05, Adriane Morabito '05-'06, John Geissler '05-'07, Tiffany Smith '06-'07, Erin Zoellick '07-'09. Ben Bishop '09-'11, Nathan Hagge '12, Jake Topp '13, and Brittany Zime '14.

In 2005, UMD began hiring full-time directors. They include Cindy Hale '05-'07, John Geissler '07-'17, and Ryan Hueffmeier '17-present.

Petersen is proud of her role in the history of the BLELC. She knows why thousands of UMD students and residents continue to enjoy Boulder Lake every year. "The place is incredible," she says.

by Cheryl Reitan

——

This banner photo was contributed by Debbie Waters Petersen. It shows her at the BLELC when she worked there in the late 1990s.

39.

UMD Helps Business Grow

Parties, businesses, a historic ice storm, and determination

Elaine Hansen was working with a lot of ingredients when she cooked up her plan to make the 25th annual Joel Labovitz Entrepreneurial Success Award Ceremony a memorable event. But, when she chose April 26, 2017, she didn't expect an ice storm.

The storm was so bad, Elaine considered canceling the event, but as the morning progressed people kept calling to say they were still coming. "If there was anything that could have gone wrong that year, it did," Elaine says.

Carol Valentini, of Valentini's Restaurant, was going to be presented with the LSBE Business Person of the Year award, and at first, many of the participants had canceled. When Carol's son walked into the hall, Carol cheered. Then, Elaine knew it was going to be alright. "It turned out to be a phenomenal event."

Elaine was the force behind making the awards so successful. "No one had ever done this before." she said. The ceremony recognized micro-entrepreneurs and emerging, established, and mature entrepreneurs. They gave a special honor to an environmentally engaged entrepreneur and a "Generations of Success Award" to honor a long-time company.

An Impactful Career

Elaine was working as the director of UMD's Center for Economic Development (CED) at the time. She also served as the regional director for the Northeast and Northwest Minnesota Small Business Development Center.

Organizing the party that day was just one of Elaine's many duties. Most of the time, she was helping to establish and grow local businesses in the Duluth area. Elaine and her staff went on hundreds of visits, from working with larger businesses like a growing aircraft company to smaller-scale enterprises such as a specialty florist.

Elaine brought a whirlwind of force to UMD and everything else that she did in her career. She was awarded the 2016 University of Minnesota President's Award for Outstanding Service, as well as the Women in Business Champion of the Year for the U.S. Small Business Administration's Minnesota District Office in 2009. The accolades were well deserved. Her assistance was shared by minority-owned and women-owned businesses and along the way, she became a role model for many.

A Bulldog Education

Before Elaine was an award-winning business woman, she was a Bulldog. Elaine says, "I graduated from Duluth Central High

School on a Friday night in 1966 and started at UMD as an undergrad the following Monday."

Elaine had planned to complete her degree in three years, but after two years, she says, "I did what all women did at the time, and got married." But, after delving into several business adventures, she returned to her UMD roots and graduated in 1980 with a B.Ac. in accounting.

She co-founded the Duluth Professional Women's Network in 1992 and served as president until 2017. Life took her to St. Paul where she took on the Commissioner of Administration position for the State of Minnesota from 1995–1999. However, this wasn't enough for Elaine and she was back in school and 2003 she graduated from UMD with her Masters in Business Administration.

A Lifetime at UMD

From student to director of UMD's CED, Elaine was a leader for women in business and she brought that leadership to all of the different roles that she played at UMD.

While working at CED, Elaine helped local businesses find financing. "We've got a vibrant business community because of our resources," she said. They can get support from the Iron Range Resources and Rehabilitation Board (IRRRB), Northland Foundation. Blandin Foundation, Arrowhead Regional Development Commission (ARDC), and Minnesota Department of Employment and Economic Development (DEED).

The CED programs provided technical assistance to between 500 and 700 businesses throughout the region each year, with more than $10,000,000 in financing, and over 300 workshops with more than 2,500 attendees in all.

These are just a few ways that Elaine paved the path for people in the Northland. Her passion to mentor and encourage others to grow and excel has proved infectious. Even though she retired in 2019, her legacy at UMD will live on.

by Izabel Johnson

——

The banner photo is Joel Labovitz (1928-2021) and Elaine Hansen at the 20th annual Joel Labovitz Entrepreneurial Success Award Ceremony. Joel Labovitz was the founder of Labovitz Enterprises, an investment firm. Previously, he was president and CEO of Maurices, the retail clothing company founded in 1931 by his father, Maurice Labovitz.

40.

Gay Pride

UMD students set the stage for human rights changes.

In 2006, a lecture hall quieted down following the influx of students at the beginning of a class. Hundreds of eyes funneled their attention to the front of the room at a small group of visitors, all members of the Queer & Allied Student Union (QASU). Among them was Chris Beasley '06.

The group was there to share their personal accounts, experience with identities, and stories about powerful and often painful experiences. One can only imagine the bravery it took to truthfully answer questions from the class.

Beasley came to UMD from rural southern Illinois. As for many people, dating websites and online chat rooms had a draw for Beasley. It was a place to explore one's sexuality and meet people of like minds. That's where he met someone who lived in Duluth and on a visit, Beasley met more people in the gay community. He described the trip to UMD as a vital part of his growth. "I experienced a revelation of possibilities," he said. "It was a 'never before felt' sense of community and connection where being gay was not reduced to secretive desires." Beasley enrolled at UMD. He pursued his undergraduate degree in psychology and also became an active member in QASU. That's also where he met the man who he would later marry. Minnesota was experiencing a shift in social change regarding LGBTQ rights during this time. Beasley and the QASU students standing in that classroom in 2006 helped explain the rapidly changing terrain.

Involved in Change

Beasley and three other QASU students, Jen Chamberlain, Molly Duepner, and Mary Van Massenhove, supported an effort by OutFront Minnesota, the states' largest LGBTQ civil rights group.

They spent many hours tabling in the Kirby Student Center and encouraging students to take an active role in their government.

According to an April 27, 2006, Statesman article, Beasley walked right up to Al Franken, at the time an Air America radio show host, who was hosting a Free Democracy Summit in the Marshall Performing Arts Center. Beasley asked him to oppose any amendment to the Minnesota Constitution that prohibits civil unions, domestic partnerships, or gay marriage.

Franken signed Beasley's petition. Beasley, who graduated at the end of the semester in 2006, set QASU on a path of civic involvement, but it would be years before a same-sex marriage effort was successful.

By 2012, when Minnesota rejected a constitutional amendment to ban same-sex marriage and 2013, when Minnesota legalized gay marriage. In June 2015, on the national front, the Supreme

Court issued another historic decision and recognized same-sex marriage.

Beasley left UMD and went on to get a master's degree from Roosevelt University and a Ph.D. from DePaul University, Chicago, and his academic pursuits have never stopped.

In 2014, he taught at Washington College in Chestertown, Maryland. In 2017, he moved to the University of Washington in Tacoma (UWT) to work on social justice and post-prison education. He co-founded the national Formerly Incarcerated College Graduates Network. They currently have 1,000 members in 43 states. Around 118 of these have or are working toward a doctorate degree. He is now leading the development of the UWT Husky Post-Prison Pathways program.

The work Beasley and QASU did in UMD's classrooms aimed to challenge the social narrative about the LGBTQ community. The advances towards equality in Minnesota were substantial.

History of LGBTQIA+ Activity at UMD

It was 1978 when the first organization Gay and Lesbian Alliance was founded on campus at UMD. Over the next forty years, this group transformed names and agendas with the progressing political climate. Ten years later, two openly LGBT professors began to make noise, speaking about the campus climate around LGBTQ issues. Lawrence Knopp, geography, and Tinke Ritmeester, woman studies, became faculty advocates. They held discussions, set up support groups, and in 1990 created the LGBT Advisory Commission.

The Gay and Lesbian Alliance was rebranded the University Gay, Lesbian and Bisexual Alliance in 1989, soon adding transgender into its acronym, ULGBTA, as well. This signaled a trend in naming conventions as it expanded to advocate for all sexual orientations. They fostered a broad coalition of queer identities to support student wellbeing and a safe place to call the organization home.

In the late 1990s, the identity of ULGBTA as an organization for advocacy and change became clear. The Statesman became filled with discourse surrounding LGBTQ issues. It was not uncommon to see the editorials filled with responses to events and issues brought up by ULGBTA, some positive and some negative.

There was no shortage of battles. ULGBTA gained community recognition in 1998 when it organized a vigil for Matthew Shepard, a gay University of Wyoming student who was the victim of a brutal attack and murder. The barbarity hate crime shocked the country and awakened many to the struggle of LGBTQ people. ULGBTA held a candlelight vigil for Matthew Shephard, an event that was recognized by the UMD's Commission on Human Diversity and the City of Duluth's Human Rights Commission.

Support staff began in 1998 with Shawn Burich, CLA staff member, and Lawrence Knopp, geography professor, staffing the Lesbian, Gay, Bisexual, Transgender (LGBT) Resource Center. A year later, students Benjamin Cruden and Karin Riggs became interim coordinators. In Spring 2000, Angie Nichols was named the Gay, Lesbian, Bisexual, and Transgender Services staff director, and in 2017, Roze Brooks took over as coordinator of Sexuality & Gender Equity Initiatives.

Back to the early 2000s. The decade began with another name rebrand, the Queer Student Union (later Queer and Allied Student Union, QASU). This decade also saw the start of many traditions for QASU. Popular events included an annual drag show and Coming Out Day luncheon. In 2007, the course CST 2001: Introduction to Gay, Lesbian, Bisexual, and Transgender Studies was offered, eventually leading to the founding of the LGBTQ Studies minor in 2015.

In 2015, a student group, called a TRANS*FORMATION was

formed to support individuals changing their gender identity, and in 2018, Queer, Trans, Intersex, Indigenous People and People of Color Collective (QTIIPOCC) was founded.

by Jack Harrington and Cheryl Reitan

———

The banner photo is from a 2015 poster for a Queer and Allied Student Union Proud Prom event called Panem Couture.

41.

UMD's Building Boom

Seven major academic buildings added prestige to UMD.

Two decades of growth gave UMD new structures that boasted state-of-the-art technology and architecturally significant design. From 1995-2010, the campus experienced a $107 million construction boom for the construction of six academic buildings, under Chancellor Kathryn A. Martin's leadership. In 2019, Chancellor Lendley Black's tenure contributed the most expensive building to date, the Heikkila Chemistry and Advanced Materials Science Building at $43 million. These seven buildings join the existing 23 academic buildings and have added to the positive reputation and prominence of UMD.

Kathryn A. Martin Library

Project Cost: $25,800,000. New Space: 136,555 gross square feet. Completion Date: September 2000

UMD's third (and current) library made its debut in 2000. It brought computers to the campus in a big way with 251 computers. This was before wifi so it also arrived with 49 laptop connections, and it soon added an additional 800 laptop connections. When the library first opened, Nate Bourassa, a junior and biology major, was quoted in the Statesman saying, "A lot of students, including myself, don't even know how to use certain computers." Luckily they all learned very quickly.

Weber Music Hall

Project Cost: $9,240,000. New Space: 25,475 gross sq ft. Completion Date: Fall 2002. Seating: 350 people. Architect: Caesar Pelli.

The Weber's tall dome shape allows a unique sound quality by sending the music up to blend together. "My first performance, as an undergrad, was in the hall in 2002 with UMD's symphony orchestra as a violinist," says Rebecca Farmer, master of music, 2012. "It was magical. The sound resonated in every corner of the space and it filled me to the bones with excitement. The year the hall opened was a year of celebration. We had so many world-renowned musicians take to the stage, including clarinetist Richard Stoltzman. When I returned to UMD for my master's in voice performance, I performed in a staged version of *Mozart's Cosi fan tutte*. It was exhilarating. For being such an intimate venue, the sound was impeccable. Just as being on stage, the sounds reverberated in a way that made you feel a part of the performance."

James I. Swenson Science Building

Project Cost: $33,000,000. New Space: 112,191 gross sq ft. Completion Date: January 2005. Architect: Ross Barney Associates

The Swenson Science Building (SSB) was named for James I. Swenson and Susan Swenson, of the Swenson Family Foundation. Jim Swenson was a 1959 chemistry graduate. The building provides facilities for the chemistry, freshwater research, and biology departments. Student Rowan Simonet says, "Thanks to the Swensons' generous contribution, UMD has a beautiful building that is perfect for academic pursuit and innovative research." Simonet, a Swenson Scholarship recipient, and 2020 biochemistry grad said, "The Swenson's gave me so much," she said. "They truly believe in the power education and science have to improve the world."

Labovitz Business and Economics Building

1949 UMD graduate Joel Labovitz and his wife, Sharon, helped fund the construction of the Labovitz Business and Economics Building. Labovitz is the founder of Labovitz Enterprises, a diversified investment firm with a focus on the hospitality industry.

Zack Filipovich, a 2012 accounting grad, remembers stepping into the Labovitz School of Business and Economics building when it first opened. "Sunlight would sparkle on the white and silver terrazzo and you knew it was going to be a good day," he says. Zack was on campus the first year of classes in the Labovitz Building. "The study rooms were perfect for group projects." Filipovich says the building motivates him to be successful. "It instilled in me a sense of opportunity, and made me believe that any challenge can be overcome with hard work and a good team."

Bagley Environmental Classroom

Project Cost: $950,000. New Space: 1400 gross sq ft. Completion Date: August 2, 2010. Architect: David Salmela

Bagley Classroom was designed to slash energy consumption as a super-insulated and airtight building. Features include passive solar heating, a high-efficiency heat recovery ventilation unit, and an on-site grid-connected solar photovoltaic system.

James I. Swenson Civil Engineering Building

Project Cost: $15,000,000. New Space: 35,000 gross sq ft. Completion Date: July, 2010. Architect: Ross Barney Associates

The American Institute of Architects named the UMD Swenson Civil Engineering building among its top-10 examples of sustainable architecture and green design solutions. This was the second building supported by the James I. Swenson Family Foundation.

Heikkila Chemistry & Advanced Materials Science Building

Project Cost: $43,100,000. New Space: 56,000 gross sq ft. Completion Date: January, 2019.

Named for donors Kurt Heikkla (1979 grad) and his wife Beth, this building supports the chemistry department and the new Chemistry & Advanced Materials Science (CAMS) Program. The fields, such as 3D printing, microelectronics, and synthetic materials development, are within the CAMS realm and the building has been called "an incubator between chemistry and engineering." 2020 graduate Michael Shea says, "UMD's recent addition of the HCAMS building to the campus has been valuable. It is an amazing building." As one of its first graduates, he has kudos for "the new, equally amazing, applied materials science master's program."

by Myka Dixon and Cheryl Reitan

____

The banner photo is of the Swenson Civil Engineering Building. It's is from the UMD University Marketing and Public Relations files.

Timeline

State Normal School, 1895 to 1921

April 2, 1895: Minnesota Governor David. M. Clough signed legislation approving the creation of the State Normal School at Duluth. The City of Duluth was required to donate six acres of land for the campus.

April 1896: Six acres of land at Twenty-third Avenue East and Fifth Street were donated by the City of Duluth and the Duluth Board of Education as a site for the new Normal School.

1897: The Minnesota State Legislature made an appropriation of $5,000 to build a foundation for the Normal School building.

1899: The Minnesota State Legislature appropriated $75,000 for erecting the "Main" building for the State Normal School at Duluth. Half of the funds were available in 1900, the rest in 1901.

February 1901: A fire left only black walls in the original "Main" building structure. The heavily insured building was reconstructed.

April 1901: Dr. Eugene W. Bohannon of the Mankato Normal School was selected as president of the State Normal School at Duluth at a salary of $2,500 per year.

September 1902: The State Normal School at Duluth started registration and operations.

June 1903: Seven women received the first diplomas granted by the State Normal School at Duluth

September 1906: Washburn Hall, a "ladies dormitory," was completed and opened. It cost $35,000.

1909: A west wing costing $60,000 was added to the Main Building.

September 1910: Torrance Hall opened as a dormitory.

1915: An east wing was added to the Main Building, and construction of the auditorium began.

1916: The State Normal School at Duluth raised its admission standards by requiring a high school diploma.

April 1921: The Normal School at Duluth was renamed the Duluth State Teachers College (DSTC).

September 1923: A four-year curriculum leading to a Bachelor of Education degree was offered for the first time.

May 1927: The new laboratory school and heating plant were dedicated.

June 1927: The first bachelor degrees were awarded at DSTC.

May 1929: The State Teachers College Board established a four-year course at DSTC. The new course qualified students for every kind of public school work.

October 1929: Less than forty men were enrolled in DSTC in 1929. By 1931, more than two hundred men were enrolled. Men remained a minority, about 20 percent, from 1931 to 1937.

December 1929: The DSTC basketball team played its first scheduled game. The team lost 38-23 to Duluth Junior College.

September 1930: DSTC played its first football game against Northland College.

January 1931: The first DSTC hockey game was played against Duluth Central High School

1933: School athletes chose the bulldog as the school's mascot.

March 1937: University of Minnesota President Lotus D. Coffman issued a document opposing branches of the University in Minnesota.

May 1937: Dr. E. W. Bohannon, 68 years old, announced his plan to retire in January.

August 1937: Dr. Herbert F. Sorenson, professor of education at the University of Minnesota, was named to succeed Bohannon. Sorenson was president from 1938 to 1946.

1937: A. I. Jedlicka wrote a bill that would require the Regents of the University of Minnesota to establish a branch in the city of Duluth.

May 1940: The last "May Fete" ceremony was held at DSTC.

1941: Olcott Hall, 23rd Avenue East and First Street, was formally accepted by DSTC. It was presented by Mrs. Dorothy Olcott Elsmith of New York and her sister, Mrs. Elizabeth Olcott Ford of La Jolla, California, daughters of J. W. Olcott, a former president of the Oliver Iron Mining Company. The home was remodeled for use as a music conservatory.

March 1946: Warren Stewart of St. Cloud, president of the State Teachers College Board, heard complaints against the administration of DSTC President Herbert Sorenson. Some faculty claimed that conditions had deteriorated since 1944. Later, "In an atmosphere charged with tension and tears," Dr. Herbert F. Sorenson announced his resignation at a special assembly. Dr. E. H. Pieper was immediately named acting president.

May 1946: Thirty-six-year-old Dr. Raymond C. Gibson, director of teachers' training at Central State Teachers College, Stevens Point, Wisconsin, was elected president of DSTC, effective July 1.

August 1946: The Minnesota State Teachers College Board approved DSTC becoming a four-year liberal arts college, beginning in the fall of 1946.

February 1947: The city planning commission reserved a vacant 160-acre diamond-shaped property west of Woodland Avenue, called the "Nortondale Tract," as a possible site for the proposed University of Minnesota branch.

February 1947: The Minnesota House began consideration of a bill by Representative A. B. Anderson for the conversion of the DSTC into a branch of the University of Minnesota.

July 1947: The name and organization of the college were changed to University of Minnesota, Duluth Branch (UMD). UMD was established as a branch college of the University of Minnesota with permission to grant the Associate in Arts, Bachelor of Arts, and Bachelor of Science degrees. Raymond C. Gibson, DSTC president, would be retained as head of UMD with the title "Provost."

August 1948: An Air Force ROTC unit was authorized for the UMD campus.

October 19, 1948: Groundbreaking ceremonies were held for the Science Building, the first building to be constructed on the "upper campus." It opened in 1951. In 1973, the name was changed to the Chemistry Building.

April 1949: Provost Gibson announced that, beginning with the 1949 summer session, graduate level courses would be offered at UMD.

June 1950: Provost Gibson announced his resignation, effective

June 30, to join the education division of the Inter-American Affairs Institute as chief administrator in Lima, Peru.

June 1951: Acting Provost John E. King, who had served in this capacity since June 1950, was appointed provost at the University Regents meeting in St. Paul on June 1, 1951.

June 1951: UMD received two large residences from Mr. and Mrs. Royal D. Alworth, Sr. The properties were located at 2605 and 2617 East Seventh Street and were adjacent to the George P. Tweed mansion (site of the first Tweed Gallery) given to UMD in 1950.

July 1951: Groundbreaking ceremonies for the Health and Physical Education Building were held. The building was occupied September 14, 1953, and was dedicated on December 12, 1953. The building was renamed Romano Gymnasium in honor of Ralph A. Romano on January 16, 1988. Total project cost: $1,602,000.

November 1951: Northeastern Minnesota civic leaders viewed "UMD-1970," a scale model of the new UMD campus plan, at Duluth's Kitchi Gammi Club. This plan, formed under the leadership of Provost King, provided the campus with the blueprint it followed for the next two decades.

June 1953: Provost King announced his resignation to accept the presidency of Kansas State Teachers College at Emporia, effective in September.

July 1953: A sixteen-acre tract of wooded land adjoining the UMD campus was given to the Board of Regents by Dr. and Mrs. William R. Bagley and their daughter Dr. Elizabeth C. Bagley. With this donation, UMD had a 196-acre campus. This gift, along with the Rock Hill gift of 1951, was dedicated as the Bagley Nature Area in 1974.

September 1953: Dr. Raymond W. Darland, academic dean and acting provost, was named UMD's third provost.

September 1953: UMD received a gift of $400,000 from Stephen R. Kirby toward the building of a student center.

October 1953: Master of Arts degrees were offered through the Graduate School at UMD.

April 1954: Groundbreaking ceremonies were held for the UMD Library. Dedication ceremonies were held February 24, 1956, with an address by Vice President Malcolm Willey.

September 1954: Groundbreaking ceremonies for the Kirby Student Center, with Stephen R. Kirby turning the first spade of earth. Kirby opened on June 21, 1956.

November 1954: Construction of Vermilion Hall began. Units were occupied in the fall of 1956.

May 1956: Groundbreaking ceremonies were held for the Humanities Building and Tweed Gallery. The new Tweed Gallery, within the Humanities Building, was dedicated in 1958. Construction began for the Mathematics-Geology Building (renamed Heller Hall on September 30, 1988). The building was completed in the spring of 1965.

September 1956: UMD joined the National Collegiate Athletic Association (NCAA).

November 1956: A campus radio station began broadcasting at 940 on the AM dial from the basement of Washburn Hall with a quarter watt of power. Call letters KUMD were officially assigned in April 1958.

April 1958: Groundbreaking ceremonies were held for the Social Science Building (renamed Cina Hall on May 4, 1958, for former University Regent Fred Cina).

May 1958: Construction for Burntside Hall began. A public open house was held a year later.

May 1958: Olcott Hall, former home of UMD's Music department since 1939, was sold.

October 1958: Tweed Gallery was officially named and dedicated.

June 1959: The Board of Regents unanimously voted to change the campus name from University of Minnesota, Duluth Branch, to the University of Minnesota, Duluth. The comma after Minnesota was used until 1999.

September 1960: Construction began for the Education Building (renamed Bohannon Hall on May 22, 1974 to honor Eugene W. Bohannon, first president of the Normal School at Duluth and Duluth State Teachers College). The dedication was held on April 11, 1962. The project was completed in the summer of 1966.

October 1960: Mrs. Alice Tweed Tuohy was the first woman honored with the University of Minnesota Regents Award.

November 1960: Construction began on the Industrial Education Building (renamed Voss-Kovach Hall on October 9, 1982). The building opened for classes in February 1962, and an official dedication was held on April 5, 1963.

February 1961: Eric Sevareid, CBS News, gave the first Dalton A. LeMasurier Memorial lecture. The lecture series honored the memory of Duluthian Dalton LeMasurier, founder of KDAL-TV.

September 1963: President John F. Kennedy addressed delegates to the Northern Great Lakes Region Conference on Land and People in the UMD Physical Education Building.

October 1964: The newly completed UMD Campus Club was dedicated.

October 1965: Construction of the Marshall W. Alworth Planetarium began. Marshall W. Alworth provided funds for the building. It was completed in the spring of 1967 and dedicated in June 1967.

November 1965: The bronze statue of French explorer Daniel Greysolon, Sieur du Lhut, created by sculptor Jacques Lipchitz, was unveiled in conjunction with the dedication of a major addition to Tweed gallery.

August 1966: Groundbreaking ceremonies for Griggs Stadium were held. The stadium was named to honor Regent Richard Griggs, who retired in 1962 after 24 years.

September 1966: Groundbreaking ceremonies for the Life Science Building were held. The building was occupied in 1968.

September 1968: UMD announced that it would sponsor the University Artist Series, a concert series featuring outstanding national and international musicians.

October 1968: Groundbreaking ceremonies were held for the Classroom-Office Building (renamed A. B. Anderson Hall in honor of prominent Duluth legislator A. B. Anderson on September 8, 1973). The building was occupied in the fall of 1970.

June 1969: Groundbreaking ceremonies were held for Lake Superior Hall. It was completed during the summer of 1971.

December 1969: Groundbreaking ceremonies were held for the Administration Building (renamed Darland Administration Building on March 12, 1982, to honor Provost Emeritus Raymond W. Darland). The building was occupied in the summer of 1971.

April 1970: Plans for apartment-style housing using prebuilt modular units (the original Village Apartments) were announced. Completion was set for the fall quarter.

July 1971: Groundbreaking ceremonies were held for the Residence Hall Dining Center. The center was occupied in July 1974.

August 1971: The Air Force ROTC program announced it would begin enrolling women in the fall of 1971.

September 1971: Groundbreaking ceremonies were held for Marshall Performing Arts Center, and the dedication was held on February 3, 1974. It was named after the parents of Julia and Caroline Marshall and Jessica Marshall Spencer (Albert and Julia N. Marshall) who were donors to the university. The Dudley Experimental Theatre (a black-box theatre within MPAC) was named for another donor, Marjorie Congdon Dudley.

November 1971: A plan to develop UMD into a major "University Center" was explained to media by Provost Darland and Vice Provost for Academic Administration David Vose. The plan envisioned the development of a School of Business, School of Fine Arts, Lake Superior Basin Studies Program, and Interdisciplinary Studies Program.

June 1972: Groundbreaking began for Stadium Apartments.

July 1972: Groundbreaking began for the Classroom-Laboratory Building (renamed Marshall W. Alworth Hall). The building was completed in the summer of 1974.

September 1972: The first class of twenty-four students at UMD School of Medicine began their program.

1973: Black Student Association established.

July 1973: Groundbreaking began for the Physical Education Field House. The building was occupied on March 10, 1975. It was named for Ward M. Wells on October 1, 1993. Wells was head of UMD's physical education department for many years.

1974: Indigenous Student Association (formerly known as the Anishinabe Club) is established.

October 1974: The Board of Regents approved UMD's academic reorganization from four divisions to two colleges and four schools: College of Letters and Science, College of Education, School of Business and Economics, School of Medicine, School of Fine Arts, and School of Social Work.

1975: The Minnesota Public Interest Research Group (student organization) is established.

February 1976: Provost Darland announced his resignation as of June 30, 1976 after 28 years at UMD, 23 of them as provost.

June 1976: Groundbreaking ceremonies were held for the UMD School of Medicine. The building was occupied on February 19, 1979, and a dedication ceremony was held on September 15.

October 1976: Groundbreaking ceremonies were held for the Health Science Library. The building was occupied in the fall of 1977.

1977: International Club (student organization) is established.

January 1977: Robert L. Heller was named provost at UMD to succeed Raymond W. Darland. Heller had been acting provost since 1976.

November 1977: University President C. Peter Magrath opened the Court Gallery at Tweed Museum of Art.

November 1977: The University of Minnesota Sea Grant Program was officially established by the National Oceanic and Atmospheric Administration (NOAA).

April 1978: Construction began on Junction Avenue Apartments (renamed Cuyuna Hall and Mesabi Hall on March 12, 1982).

1979: Women's Resource and Action Center is established.

January 1979: The combined estates of brothers Jonathan, Simon, and Milton Sax were bequeathed to the Tweed Museum of Art. A one million dollar gift for the purchase of original artworks came from the Milton Sax estate. Paintings, sculpture, and other artworks were to be purchased from the interest of the "Simon, Milton, and Jonathan Sax Purchase Fund." In 1987, the Sax gift funded construction of the Sax Gallery, a sculpture conservatory.

May 1979: The Northern Bible Society of Duluth presented UMD with one of the largest Bible collections in the U.S.

July 1979: Glensheen, the 39-room Congdon mansion that was gifted to the University of Minnesota, was opened to public tours for the first time. In the first five days, 3,800 persons toured the mansion and grounds.

October 1979: Groundbreaking ceremonies were held for the School of Business and Economics Building. The building was occupied in the fall of 1981 and the dedication was held on March 7, 1982.

September 1980: The first Study-in-England group of students left for a year at the University of Birmingham in England.

October 1980: The Duluth chapter of the Minnesota Education Association (UMDEA) became the first faculty bargaining unit in a runoff election with American Association of University Professors (AAUP).

November 1980: Groundbreaking ceremonies were held for Oakland Avenue Apartments (individually named Oak, Aspen, Birch, and Basswood Halls).

July 1983: The Natural Resources Research Institute (NRRI) was created by Governor Rudy Perpich, Minnesota legislators, and community leaders.

March 1984: UMD's hockey Bulldogs won the WCHA title by defeating North Dakota 12-6.

September 1984: Establishment of the annual Albert Tezla Scholar/ Teacher Award was announced by Donald K. Harriss, vice provost for academic administration.

1985: UMD's American Indian Learning Resource Center opens.

June 1986: Chancellor Heller announced his retirement from the University, effective June 30, 1987.

July 1986: NRRI reached an agreement with the U.S. Steel mineral research laboratory at Coleraine. The agreement included the sale of laboratory and research equipment at the Coleraine facility and the lease of portions of land, several buildings, and some mobile equipment.

December 1986: The new Engineering Building opened.

May 1987: UMD's theatre production *Homesteaders* was judged best in the region and was selected by the American College Theatre Festival to be performed at the Kennedy Center in Washington, D.C. A second production, *Blue Collar Blues*, also won both awards in 1989 and a third production, *Standing on My Knees*, won both awards again in 1991.

July 1987: Lawrence A. Ianni took office as chancellor at UMD. Ianni was formerly provost and vice president for academic affairs at San Francisco State University.

June 1989: A complex of three new UMD residence halls was named Goldfine Hall at a dedication ceremony honoring Erwin L. Goldfine, who served twelve years on the Board of Regents before retiring in 1987.

1990: Latinx/Chicanx Student Association (formerly known as the Hispanic Organization) is established.

1991: The UMD Athletic Hall of Fame is established. It now consists of 140 distinguished members, representing 21 sports.

1991: Asian Pacific Student Association (formerly known as Southeast-Asian-American Student Organization) is established.

1991: SERVE (student organization) is established.

1993: Access for All (student organization) established.

February 1993: Old Main, UMD's original building on the lower campus built at the turn of the century, was destroyed in an arson fire the night of February 22. The site later was donated to the City of Duluth for a park.

May 1993: The School of Medicine, Duluth campus, was selected for a special recognition achievement award by the American Academy of Family Physicians.

May 1994: Chancellor Ianni announced he would step down after serving as UMD's chancellor since 1987.

September 1994: A Library Building task force was appointed. The task force sought support to erect a new library building.

November 1994: President Bill Clinton appeared at a political rally at UMD.

March 1995: A 100-year birthday celebration for UMD was held in MPAC.

October 1995: The new UMD Campus Center was dedicated "The Wedge." A separate dedication for the Campus Center sculptures, "Untitled," commissioned from Minneapolis sculptor Steven Woodward, was held in the Campus Center plaza.

November 1995: Kathryn A. Martin, formerly dean of the College of Fine and Applied Arts at the University of Illinois at Urbana,

Champaign, was inaugurated as eighth chancellor of the University of Minnesota Duluth. She is the first woman chancellor in the University of Minnesota system.

1997: UMD purchased a vessel built in 1985 for fishing on the Grand Banks. The *Blue Heron* is converted into a limnological research vessel during the winter of 1997–98 and outfitted with state-of-the-art research equipment with berthing for 11 crew and scientists.

1999: The comma was dropped and the university's name becomes the University of Minnesota Duluth.

1999: Queer and Allied Student Union (formerly known as University Lesbian Gay Bisexual Transgender Alliance) is established.

September 2000: UMD's new library, designed by Duluth architect Ken Johnson, SJA, opened. The building, comprised of 167,570 gross square feet, cost $26 million. A glass sculpture by Dale Chihuly hangs from the ceiling of the two-story library lobby.

March 25, 2001: The Women's Hockey team earned the NCAA Division I national championship by defeating St. Lawrence University with a score of 4–2.

2002: The Women's Hockey team won its second NCAA Division I national by defeating Brown University with a score of 3–2.

October 2002: Weber Music Hall, designed by world-famous architect Cesar Pelli, cost $9.2 million. It was funded, in part, by a generous donation from Mary Ann and Ron Weber, who met at UMD while they were students.

2003: The Women's Hockey team won its third NCAA Division I national championship, defeating Harvard University with a score of 4–3, in double overtime.

2004: The Multicultural Center opened. Its mission is to enhance academic achievement, create a sense of belonging, celebrate diversity, and foster positive relations among UMD students, faculty and staff. The Oromo Student Association is established.

September 2005: The James I. Swenson Science Building, designed by Carol Ross Barney, Ross Barney Associates, Chicago, Illinois, opened. The 110,000 gross square-foot building was named for alumnus Jim Swenson '59, who together with his wife, Susan, made a generous donation to fund the building.

June 2006: The 80-foot-tall steel sculpture *Wild Ricing Moon* by sculptor John David Mooney was installed on the lawn across from the Swenson Science Building.

September 2006: The 46,000 gross square-foot UMD Sports and Health Center opened. In spring 2001, UMD students voted to contribute $4 million toward the center. The Minnesota Legislature then authorized $8.4 million in spring 2005 to complete the project. It was designed by RDG Planning & Design.

2007: National Society of Black Engineers is established.

2008: The Women's Hockey team won its fourth NCAA Division I national championship, defeating the University of Wisconsin, 4–0.

2008: The Labovitz School of Business and Economics was named for the Labovitz family: alumnus Joel, his wife Sharon, and their three children. Their generous gift paved the way for further legislative funding. The total cost of the facility was $23 million. It was designed by Ralph E. Johnson, Perkins+Will, Chicago, Illinois.

December 13, 2008: The undefeated Bulldogs won the NCAA Division II National Football Championship, defeating Northwest Missouri State.

September 3, 2009: Chancellor Kathryn A. Martin announced her retirement, effective July 31st, 2010.

July 31, 2010: The Women's Hockey team won its fifth NCAA Division I national championship, defeating Cornell with a score of 3–2, in triple overtime.

2010: The James I. Swenson Engineering Building opened. It houses UMD's civil engineering program. The building was funded, in part, by Jim and Susan Swenson. The total cost of the building was $15 million and was designed by Carol Ross Barney, Ross Barney Associates, Chicago, Illinois. 2010: Bagley Classroom, designed as a multi-purpose space for all UMD Departments, was designed by Duluth architect David Salmela.

August 1, 2010: Lendley C. Black began his tenure as the ninth chancellor of UMD. Before becoming UMD's chancellor, he served as provost and vice president for academic affairs at Kennesaw State University in Kennesaw, Georgia.

December 18, 2010: The Football team won their second Division II national title, defeating Delta State 20–17.

April 9, 2011: The Men's Hockey team defeated the University of Michigan, 3–2 in overtime, to win its first NCAA Division I Championship.

October 7, 2013: The UMD Library is renamed the Kathryn A. Martin Library in honor of former Chancellor Martin.

2017: Hmong Living in Unity and Balance (student organization) is established.

April 7, 2018: The Men's Hockey team captured its second national championship with a 2–1 win over the University of Notre Dame.

April 13, 2019: The Men's Hockey team captured its third championship (and second consecutive one), with a 3–0 win over the University of Massachusetts Amherst.

August 9, 2019: The three story, 56,000 sq. ft. Heikkila Chemistry and Advanced Materials Science building held its grand opening. It is named for benefactors Kurt and Beth Heikkila. The HCAMS building is the home of the Heikkila Advanced Materials Center.

October 14, 2019: UMD formalizes a Land Acknowledgment statement to recognize its location on tribal land. The Land Acknowledgment was endorsed by the Minnesota Indian Affairs Council on June 4, 2019.

———

Dates on this timeline prior to 1996 were gathered from *UMD Comes of Age. Moran, K. & Storch, N. (1996)*. Virginia Beach: Donner Company.

Acknowledgements

The University of Minnesota Duluth *(UMD)* appreciates all of the students, staff, and faculty who worked on this volume. This book was written during UMD's 125th anniversary from January 2020 to 2021.

Cheryl Reitan, the associate director for University Marketing and Public Relations (UMPR) was responsible for the inception and the execution of *Stories from the Past: The Rare and Remarkable.* She took the book from web pages, to inclusion in the Alumni E-newsletter, and finally to the publication of this book.

The following students contributed immensely to the project, beginning with Ellie Mercil. Additional students helped with writing and production including: Myka Dixon, Sara Guymon, Jack Harrington, Bailey Jacobson, Izabel Johnson, Maija Johnson, Jessica Leung, Eva Moua, and Jack Wiedner. The UMPR staff supported the project, including Charlene Aaseng, David Cowardin, Brett Groehler, Hannah Lieberman, Kyle Marxhausen, Kathleen McQuillan-Hoffman, and Lynne Williams. Lori C. Melton, UMPR senior communication specialist, wrote and edited stories. Aimee Brown and Shana Aue, staff at the UMD Archives and Special Collections, Kathryn A. Martin Library, were especially helpful during the creation of this collection. Special thanks to Professor David Beard for his encouragement.

Images

Front Cover: (Clockwise From Upper Left) Swenson Civil Engineering Building, Floor Detail in Kirby Student Center, Floor detail in Cina Hall, and the Old Main arches.